The End Times
The Book of Revelation, Antichrist 666, Tribulation, Armageddon and the Return of Jesus Christ

Doomsday Apocalypse in
the Last Days of Earth
The Millennial Reign,
Apostate Church &
the Messianic Age

Paul Backholer

The End Times: The Book of Revelation, Antichrist 666, Tribulation, Armageddon and the Return of Jesus Christ.

Scripture quotations are taken from:
- NKJV – The New King James Version. Published by Thomas Nelson, Inc. Copyright © 1982 by Thomas Nelson, Inc. Used by permission. All rights reserved.
- Scriptures taken from the Holy Bible, New International Version®, NIV®. Copyright © 1973, 1978, 1984, 2011 by Biblica, Inc.™ Used by permission of Zondervan. All rights reserved worldwide. www.zondervan.com The "NIV" and "New International Version" are trademarks registered in the United States Patent and Trademark Office by Biblica, Inc.™
- AV – Authorised Version / King James Version.

ISBN 978-1-907066-86-3
British Library Cataloguing In Publication Data. A Record of this Publication is available from the British Library.

First published in 2022 by ByFaith Media

- Jesus Christ is Lord -

Book Themes

* Jesus on the Last Days
* The Key to the End Times
* Six End of the Age Signs
* Israel and the Jews
* Church Apostasy
* Holy Spirit Awakening
* 666 – Mark of the Beast
* The Third Jewish Temple
* Media Bias and Antichrist
* Preparation for One World Government
* Work of Antichrist spirits and Signs of the Times
* Foundations for the Man of Sin
* Censorship to Prepare for Antichrist
* Escaping the Seven Year Tribulation
* The Rapture of the Church of Jesus
* The Divided Tribulation Explained
* Seven Seals and Seven Trumpets
* Seven Thunders and Seven Bowls of Wrath
* Antichrist's Peace Treaty with Israel
* Four Horses of the Apocalypse
* The Jews and the 144,000 Evangelists
* Antichrist Smashes Israel's Peace Treaty
* War on Israel and the Invasion of Jerusalem
* Abomination of Desolation, Temple Defiled
* War on the Saints and Persecution of the Jews
* The Counterfeit Antichrist Resurrection
* The Meaning of the Beast from the Earth
* Supernatural Power and the Beast out of the Sea
* Two Supernatural Witnesses, Elijah and Moses
* Armageddon Apocalypse, Nuclear War
* Restoration of the Jews to the Messiah
* Return of Jesus Christ, Every Eye Will See Him
* Millennial Reign on Earth, Perfect Peace
* Devil Bound for a Thousand Years
* The Total Defeat of Satan and the Demonic
* Great White Throne Judgment
* The Nephilim and Antichrist
* The End of Earth in Fire
* New Heaven, New Earth

Contents

Thus says the Lord,
the Holy One of Israel and his Maker,
"Ask Me of things to come concerning My sons and
concerning the work of My hands"
(Isaiah 45:11).

I am God and there is none like Me, declaring
the end from the beginning and from ancient times
things that are not yet done, saying, "My counsel
shall stand and I will do all My pleasure"
(Isaiah 46:9-10).

Watch therefore, for you know neither the
day nor the hour in which the Son of Man is coming
(Matthew 25:13).

And to wait for His Son from Heaven, whom He
raised from the dead, even Jesus who
delivers us from the wrath to come
(1 Thessalonians 1:10).

For God did not appoint us to wrath, but to
obtain salvation through our Lord Jesus Christ
(1 Thessalonians 5:9).

Watch therefore and pray always that you
may be counted worthy to escape all these
things that will come to pass and to
stand before the Son of Man
(Luke 21:36).

Chapter One

The Creation of the World

Nobody believes it's going to happen until it does. That's what the coronavirus pandemic taught us. The unbelievable will take place. It is prophesied. Pandemics spread, civilisations end, empires crumble and life as we know it, will cease. Don't let time deceive you into thinking we are immune. The Roman Empire fell after more than a thousand years and the Soviet Union collapsed within sixty-nine. All which has a beginning must end.

It was late on the Lord's Day and in the Spirit, I saw a limitless ladder rising into the sky. A voice said, "Come up here." I climbed and the ladder reached through the cloud into the nothingness above. Then a hand caught hold and pulled me into the bleak darkness above (Genesis 28:12, Revelation 4:1).

Suddenly, a bright light shot past and flew across what I now recognised as an empty universe. In the far distance, there was a rush of sound and I saw a planet forming. Bursts of light appeared in every direction until the darkness gave way to the sight of planets and their moons being assembled.

Clusters of stars, constellations, and planets of all shapes and sizes grew, and aged at speed. I was in silence as a meteorite of bright light flew straight past me into the endless realms of space. The universe was being breathed into existence and I gave thanks to God. It was power and beauty combined.

With light glimmering from the stars, there was a dark planet in the distance. It was void, without form and was covered with water, and darkness was on the face of the deep. It was earth. A light shone over the planet, like a curtain of glory being pulled across it. The light was from the Word and the Word was light, and the planet burst into life (John 1:1-3, 8:12).

The earth shook and trembled in power. There was a universal earthquake and out of this burst of energy, mountain tops emerged and peaked. Following abruptly land masses and continents developed. Beams of light like the trail of a shooting star crossed in every direction on earth and grass, trees, and vegetation grew in haste.

Above, the sun emerged expanding out of the blackness of nothing, blowing up like a balloon. It was bright, rich in colour – golden, with yellow and red, and exploding with power. It appeared young (Genesis 1:14).

In the universe, stars and planets moved by Divine command, aligning themselves together to designate times and seasons, and then I saw it. There was a natural satellite of earth, which I knew by the name Moon, and the sea on the planet moved with its gravitational pull. On earth, the sea commenced teaming with life and animals appeared over the land, from rabbits to cattle, as the breath of God created all.

My spiritual eyes opened and I was now one of many in a crowd. An angelic host without number stood before God singing in praise and worship. With every mighty act, the angels produced a sound of adoration. At the heart of the congregation of angels sat God the Father and Jesus Christ beside, and the Holy Spirit hovered over the face of the waters (Genesis 1:2).

"Time without time, space without space," I heard in my spirit.

The Lord Jesus Christ, dressed in white with fire bursting from His eyes, held His right hand high, as the three members of the Trinity spoke in unison, with the sound of many waters, "Let Us make man in Our image" (Genesis 1:2, 26, Job 26:13, 33:4, Psalm 104:30, John 1:1-4, 14, Colossians 1:15-17, Hebrews 1:2-31, John 1:1, Revelation 19:13).

A voice cried out, "For by Him all things were created that are in Heaven and on earth, visible and invisible, whether thrones or dominions or principalities or powers. All things were created through Him and for Him. All things were made through Him and without Him nothing was made that was made. In Him was life and the life was the light of men. And the light shines in the darkness and the darkness did not comprehend it. By faith we understand that the worlds were framed by the Word of God, so that the things which are seen were not made of things which are visible" (John 1:3-5, Colossians 1:16, Hebrews 11:3).

With an angelic host watching, the Lord God formed man from the dust and breathed into his nostrils the breath of life, and man became a living being. An angel celebrated, saying, "God Almighty, in whose hand is the life of every living thing and the breath of all people" (Genesis 2:7, Job 12:10).

There was silence and the angels turned to me. These words ushered forth, "The Spirit of God has made me and the breath of the Almighty gives me life," and they nodded in agreement (Job 33:4, Ezekiel 37:10).

Everything was being observed in fast forward. I saw the first man and woman on earth, and the sound of thunder broke in the Heavenlies as Adam and Eve were thrown out of God's presence. Creation groaned as sin entered the world. Their sons fought and one was killed. It was the first murder, followed by many more. I looked away in shame. We trampled glory in our sin (Genesis 4:8, Romans 8:22).

Mankind multiplied on earth and became more wicked and the Spirit of God strived with them in righteousness. A flood followed submerging the planet, with an Ark of salvation floating above the judgment and the world rested for a moment from its iniquities. The great rainbow faded as towns, cities and nations birthed, growing and expanding. A tower grew with men like ants building it up to Heaven until it fell and the people scattered (Genesis 6:3-4).

In the Heavenlies, the Trinity spoke to each other and they called Abram. From the seed of Abram came the patriarchs, prophets, priests, kings, nations and the Messiah (Genesis 12:2, 22:18).

The promise to Abram was barely spoken when events moved with haste. Lot ran from Sodom and Gomorrah, as fire and brimstone rained down upon them. He was saved from the judgment which fell from Heaven.

Then a voice spoke in thunder with lightning, "As it was

in the days of Noah, so it will be also in the days of the Son of Man: They ate, they drank, they married wives, they were given in marriage, until the day that Noah entered the ark, and the flood came and destroyed them all. Likewise, as it was also in the days of Lot: They ate, they drank, they bought, they sold, they planted, they built, but on the day that Lot went out of Sodom it rained fire and brimstone from Heaven and destroyed them all. Even so, will it be in the day when the Son of Man is revealed" (Luke 17:26-30).

Chapter Two

An Outcry

In a moment all was silent and change ceased. It was present day and I was above the earth in the Spirit looking down. In the distance was a hazy white mist and a figure emerged.

"It's you," I said in a whisper, with a warm smile, "The angel with no name, who showed me Heaven."

"I have a name," replied the angel, "but it's too great for you to know."

"You look different," I stated.

"The Lord wants you to listen and share what you hear."

"I am the Lord's servant," I said.

"You have been called here to witness and testify. You must listen to all you hear and search the Scriptures. For the prince of the power of the air deceives the world. Many have claimed to have seen Heaven and the end times, and yet their descriptions are contrary to God's written Word; it cannot be so with you!" (Isaiah 34:16, Ephesians 2:2).

"I want to walk in the truth," I confessed.

"What you are about to see you must weigh," said the angel. "Only the Bible is trustworthy. The power of God's Word must test all; never trust a revelation which contradicts it."

"A prophecy of the future!" I replied.

"With a prophetic word God's servants declare, 'Thus says the Lord,' and it will be. This is not such a time. You will not receive a timeline of forthcoming events. I will show you signs and seasons. You will see what is past, echoes of the present and signs for the future. We will show you what could be, but the Church has the power to change events through prayer" (Ephesians 6:12).

"What!" I exclaimed, stunned by the concept.

"When the Church prays and births a spiritual awakening, the enemy is restrained," said the angel. "By plundering Hell, the Antichrist is held back because those who would have supported him are redeemed. The witness of the Holy Spirit in the Church is restraining the enemy" (2 Thessalonians 2:6-7).

"I fear those who say we can get out of balance when we focus on the end times," I confessed.

"Seven is the number of perfection," said the angel, "and there are seven noble reasons why the Church must understand the end times. Do not fear those who are blinded by 'their own' doctrines.

"The first is because God wants the Church to know what will happen in the future. Passages in the Bible concerning the end times must be read, studied and understood. The Bible says, 'Surely the Lord God does nothing unless He reveals His secret to His servants the prophets.' Therefore the Almighty does not want His people to be ignorant: Remember, 'the Lord God of the holy prophets sent His angel to show His servants the things which must shortly take place' (Amos 3:7, Revelation 22:6).

"The second is because Jesus commands His Church to watch for the signs of the times in their pursuit of holiness. The Lord said, 'Watch therefore and pray always that you may be counted worthy to escape all these things that will come to pass, and to stand before the Son of Man' (Luke 21:36).

"The third is to restrain the antichrist spirit and bring in a great harvest for the Kingdom of God. Every born again believer who prays and votes with Kingdom principles will slow the rise of the Antichrist. God has a trump card in each generation who will fight against forming a union of nations against Christ. By resisting, souls will be saved (2 Thessalonians 2:6).

"The fourth is to protect believers from deception, who live during the rise of the Man of Sin. Many will celebrate the coming of Antichrist and receive the Mark of the Beast. Christians who walk in discernment will resist and be saved from the wrath to come (1 Thessalonians 1:10, 5:9).

"The fifth is to teach you God is sovereign. The Antichrist will not rise because the Almighty cannot stop him. He will rise because the Lord will give the unbelieving nations exactly what they want. They will learn the horror of a world without the Almighty protecting them. The Bible says, 'For this reason God will send them a strong delusion, that they should believe the lie' (2 Thessalonians 2:11).

"The sixth is to inspire Christians to fulfil the Great Commission. Every tribe, tongue, people and nation must hear the gospel (Matthew 24:14, Titus 2:11-13).

"The seventh is because God promises a blessing on all who read and keep the words of His prophecy in the Book of Revelation. To escape the rule of Antichrist is a blessing indeed!" (Revelation 1:3, 22:7).

"This is heavy teaching," I said.

"Now you know the rise of the Antichrist can be restrained. For this reason, you must accept you will see what can be, but not all of what will be. The world moves at a pace and events unfold. Those who pray can restrain the evil and postpone its revelation. Believers who press in for revival can turn hearts back to Christ and slow the plans of the enemy. In all your seeing, see this, only Scripture tells you what will come to pass."

"Help me understand," I pleaded.

"Be still and think upon all that God wants you to know. You have seen creation, and you have watched as mankind became corrupt and lost in sin. You have seen thousands of years of history and yet in the eyes of God, all you have witnessed is a few days! Soon the end is to come upon mankind. For with the Lord, one day is as a thousand years and a thousand years as one day (2 Peter 3:8).

"In the Heavenlies we have heard the voices of scoffers, walking according to their own lusts, saying, 'Where is the promise of His coming?' We hear them complain, the fathers of the faith have fallen asleep and all things continue as they were from the beginning of creation. But this they wilfully forget: that by the Word of God the Heavens were of old and the world that then existed perished, being flooded with water. You have heard of Noah and you have seen him from afar. Now, in your time and generation, the Heavens and the earth are still preserved by the same Word of Christ's power. They are reserved for fire until the Day of Judgment and perdition of ungodly men" (2 Peter 3:7, 10).

"Open my eyes," I implored.

"God's angels hear the cries of the suffering saints far from your lands, saying, 'How long must we wait for redemption?' Now, the Lord is not slack concerning His promise, as some count slackness, but is longsuffering, not willing that any should perish in Hell, but that all should come to repentance" (2 Peter 3:3-9).

"You bring favourable news," I said, in hope.

"The gospel is good news, but many refuse to hear," the angel announced, and he added something which struck cold. "Your world has become an enemy of God."

"God is merciful and gracious," I declared, with folded arms. "He would never become the enemy of this world."

"I did not tell you God is your enemy, I told you your world has become an enemy of God. You lived through the coronavirus pandemic, yet how many honestly turned to the Lord with all their heart and soul? They chose every other option before God; they put their faith in all else before thinking of the Lord."

I sighed, agreeing.

"God is holy," the angel announced.

"I know," I replied.

"You believe you understand what this means, but you do not understand. God is holy. He is not part holy, or someone who loves holiness. He is holy and His absolute holiness demands He hates all unrighteousness. Those who are at war with righteousness have made themselves enemies of God. They have declared war on Him and He will soon respond!"

"I fear such talk," I confessed. "I wish for Him to blanket us with His love."

"He is, but it would be impossible for Him to be holy without hating sin," the angel said. "All unrighteousness is an affront to Him. His holy nature confirms He will always hate sin. If unrighteousness was acceptable to Him, He would not be holy. God Almighty loves the world, but to be an adversary of all that is holy, is to be an enemy of God" (Romans 8:7, James 4:4).

"I understand," I replied.

I was lifted in the Spirit to another place above earth, where I saw the planet. Encircling it was a thin blue glow, and I saw ample clouds covering vast areas and weather systems moving. It was a glorious experience (Ezekiel 8:3).

I thought the earth was exceptionally beautiful, as I considered the billions of stories unfolding. Families were singing, dancing, learning, laughing, joking, walking, swimming, meeting, talking, praying and falling in love. It amazed me, as I thought of all the possibilities of these developing stories.

"It is wonderful," I said.

"Would you like to listen to what we hear in Heaven from earth?"

I imagined myself as a Heavenly spy, listening to a thousand stories of miracles. "Yes please," I said.

I looked on the earth and saw in the Spirit a noise coming towards me in the shape of a cloud of voices. The first stage of the sound penetrated my consciousness with horror. The mixture of the outcry I heard was of sirens from the police, ambulance and fire vehicles. Then, the terror of a million screams.

The sun was setting on the United States and behold, horror and great darkness fell upon me. The light shining in my spirit was covered with a dark blanket of reality. Fear struck me from without and fears birthed within (Genesis 15:12, 2 Corinthians 7:5).

I heard the modern sound of Jeremiah's fear. The angel gazed at me and I was given insight to distinguish between voices. I heard the cries of the victims of ungodly sinners – the unholy, profane, murderers, manslayers, fornicators, kidnappers, liars, perjurers, the cowardly, unbelieving, sexually immoral, sorcerers and idolaters (Jeremiah 9:1-26, 1 Timothy 1:9-10, Revelation 21:8).

"The horror," I thought.

Just a few minutes ago I imagined the world as a place of love, romance and beauty. Now, I heard the cries of injustice. Men used men for profit; they bought and sold people, used and abused God's creation. Endless spiritual clouds, getting thicker each time, rose from earth and thrust into the Heavenlies, filled with news of wave upon wave of evil. I heard the inner heart cries of 'the good people' spilling out hatred, anger, bitterness and vice. It was a world of hate, crime, abuse, injustice and sin.

They called good evil and evil good. Light was now darkness and darkness light. Bitter was sweet and sweet was bitter. I saw media images of every sin imagined; I heard politicians and celebrities using clever words to defend their right to use and abuse others. A voice said, "Not even a pandemic will make them repent and turn their hearts to the Lord" (Isaiah 5:20).

Following sharply was the sound of genocide, wars, starvation, abortion, sexual abuse, violence, drunkenness and hatred. There were cries of oppression, theft, low pay and exorbitant bills. A minority possessed more than half the world's wealth combined. Those with private jets, mansions and obese luxury ignored the plight of the billions going to sleep in hunger. It sounded like screams combined.

The weight of the burden was crushing. "Make it stop," I pleaded. "Make it stop!"

The screams ceased and I was left in silence in a deep state of despair. I was silent for some time, numb with pain. Then, I stared blankly towards earth in growing anger, as deep distress overcame me.

"Take me to Heaven now," I said. "How can I blindly continue having heard the cry of hundreds of millions of aborted babies from China, India, the West and the East? How can you stand to hear such evil cries?"

"It's not a wonderful world," said the angel, with a gentle tone, "it's a world of hidden horror. This is what it means to hear an outcry from earth about the sins of mankind" (Genesis 18:20-21, 19:13).

"It is an evil sound," I confessed, my hands still shaking.

"We heard the outcry of Sodom and Gomorrah, and you know how God moved to end the sin. The Almighty must act again and release the burden of the prophets: 'I am restless in my complaint…because of the oppression of the wicked. My heart is severely pained within me and the terrors of death have fallen upon me, and horror has overwhelmed me. The earth – destruction is in its midst, oppression and deceit do not depart from its streets' " (Psalm 55:2-5, 11, 2 Peter 2:6, Jude 7).

"Doom is ahead," I began to accept.

"Do not be confused," said the angel. "The goodness of God leads to repentance. God is gracious and merciful, slow to anger and abundant in loving kindness, and He relents from doing harm. He has been merciful and slow to anger in your time, and yet the nations refuse to repent and respond to His mercy" (Jonah 4:2, Romans 2:4).

"Forgive us," I implored.

"Instead of thanking Him for giving them time to repent," replied the angel, "they have taken this period of grace, as a sign that Heaven ignores their sin. King Solomon foresaw this when he said, 'Because the sentence against an evil work is not executed speedily, therefore the heart of the sons of men is fully set in them to do evil' (Ecclesiastes 8:11).

"The more grace God sends to earth, the more sin abounds to the harm of all. Just think of the harm man now does to man. The world is blind to the misery it inflicts on others and when you consume media, you see the world as your culture wants you to see it, not as it really is. The hidden suffering is covered by the culture which has indoctrinated humanity to accept sin. You don't know the pain of always hearing millions of cries of horror in each moment. You live amid a crooked and perverse generation. You live in an age that drinks iniquity like water and they have hardened their spirit against God. As Isaiah warned, the whole heart of your civilisation is sick and there is no soundness" (Job 15:13-16, Isaiah 1:5-6, Philippians 2:15).

I quietly absorbed this shock. In the stillness, anger arose within. My naivety of how bad things are was being replaced with a growing anger.

"Smite it with fire," I declared, in the flesh. "Save those who are saved, deliver the innocent and punish the evil. End this misery once and for all!"

"You do not know what manner of spirit you are of," the angel said, with feet astride in power. "The son of Man did not come to destroy men's lives, but to save them" (Luke 9:55-56).

I calmed down and retreated. The sound of evil created anger in me, but in Heaven, it drew compassion for the victims and a desire for redemption.

"Do you not understand the burden of Amos?" the angel asked. "Woe to you who desire the Day of the Lord, for what good is the Day of the Lord to you? It will be darkness and not light" (Amos 5:18).

I didn't know what to say. I felt more like the son of Adam, than a child of the King of kings. As I chastised myself in my soul, a Scripture came to heart: 'My son, do not despise the chastening of the Lord, nor be discouraged when you are rebuked by Him. For whom the Lord loves He chastens and scourges every son whom He receives' (Hebrews12:5-6).

"You think the end times are something to be feared," said the angel, "but when this world ends, it will silence the misery, the corruption and the cries of the innocent, who are abused in their millions. Every judgment which befalls humanity will be just" (Hebrews 2:2).

"But the righteous will suffer with the innocent," I replied.

"No, the righteous will be saved. Like Noah and his family, they will be saved from destruction. You have heard the sound of the abused for a moment and your flesh cried for destruction. But God has heard these cries for thousands of years and He must act. His righteous judgment demands action and He will save the just and punish the unjust. You are fearful the good will die, but the Lord is good. The Bible says, 'The righteous perish and no man takes it to heart. Merciful men are taken away, while no one considers that the righteous is taken away from evil. He shall enter peace' (Isaiah 57:1-2).

"You have forgotten all flesh is as grass, all will die and face the judgment. In the end times, God will speed up the process and all will face reality before it's too late" (1 Peter 1:24).

"Will God give them a chance to be saved before the end?" I inquired.

"He has, is and will give them many chances to respond to the call, for whosoever will, can come to Christ. If you are willing to hear, listen to this: The Tribulation will confront millions with the claims of Heaven and Hell on their soul. God will use a series of judgments to bring a multitude into the Kingdom of God" (Revelation 7:9-17).

"Oh Lord, have mercy," I thought.

"The Tribulation means terror for those with hard hearts, but salvation to those who are willing to respond to Christ. Many know about Christianity, but few have truly heard the gospel of Christ's love. Remember the words of Isaiah: 'For behold, the Lord takes away from Jerusalem and from Judah the stock and the store, the whole supply of bread and the whole supply of water.' Do you understand why?" (Isaiah 3:1).

"No," I confessed.

"God credited short-term suffering as worthwhile, if it leads to repentance and eternal salvation. It is an act of mercy to save souls and force a response from lost sinners, unwilling to listen in their former prosperity. Listen to the Word of the Lord through the prophets: 'In their affliction, they will earnestly seek Me,' and the voice of the saved will say, 'It was good for me that I have been afflicted, that I may learn' " (Psalm 119:71, Hosea 5:15).

"Salvation first," I confessed.

"John saw a great multitude which no one could number of all nations, tribes, peoples and tongues, standing before the throne. He asked, 'Who are these arrayed in white robes and where did they come from?' The reply, 'These are the ones who come out of the Great Tribulation, and washed their robes and made them white in the blood of the Lamb' (Revelation 7:9-10, 13-14).

"Many will turn to the ultimate Good, as the burden of eternity is made real by the end of all things. There are billions who are unwilling to heed God's voice and come to Christ. They must be awoken out of their sleep, to give them one last chance to repent and be saved.

"The coming Tribulation will lead to the salvation of a great multitude that no one can number, it is mercy and judgment intertwined. Mercy and truth have met together, righteousness and peace will kiss. It is the truth of Hell made palpable by the kiss of eternal life" (Psalm 85:10).

Chapter Three

Babylon Must Fall

I saw New York City and a meteorite flew down from the sky smashing into buildings. People ran into the streets in a state of bewilderment and sirens echoed throughout the city. Simultaneously, an earthquake rocked Asia and skyscrapers in Hong Kong toppled into Victoria Harbour. In Australia, Sydney Opera House collapsed and in England, Big Ben shook.

"This is terrible," I thought, in disbelief.

"What happens when you face a crisis?" asked the angel. "You turn to God like never before. You pray as you never pray and the eternal realm becomes real."

"But the cost!" I said.

"The end times are a wake-up call to face reality. They are God's mercy expressed in His greatest trumpet sound. To be left asleep when the house is on fire is not kindness. To be shaken out of bed, thrown out if necessary is tough love in action. Mankind has to lose its temporal hope to gain eternal life. This is the purpose of the end times."

"Oh gosh," I sighed.

"Think about it. Your generation has tried to hide death out of sight; youth is worshipped and old age is shunned. In previous generations people died younger, and everyone was aware of their mortality and the call of eternity. They fell on their knees because in life there is death. The coming end time judgments will restore the fear of eternity without Christ."

"Mercy, I pray."

"Eternal peace and joy can only be found in the full redemption of Christ," said the angel. "It is merciful to cause the world to lose a few short years to disaster, to help them find an endless supply of eternal life. Seven years of Tribulation to save them from an eternity in Hell!

"Sometimes a loving father has to cut off his rich

children, to teach them the value of all they have. Without this awakening, his children will squander their lives and will fall into the mire. There is no joy in the pigpen of judgment, but there is salvation! This is the prodigal generation and it needs the medicine given to the prodigal son to turn them to God!" (Luke 15:11-32).

"Oh Lord...another way," I sighed.

"When the economy crashes and meteorites fall from the sky, people will forget all the distractions they love," explained the angel. "All their hope in celebrities will fall; their trust in their investments will crash and passion for politics will dissolve. No man will be able to solve this crisis. When the world is shaking under their feet, people will pray!"

"God help us," I groaned, speaking slowly.

"There is great deception in wealth," said the angel, "they think all is well. You are living in the modern Sodom and Gomorrah. Listen to what Jesus said, 'In the days of Lot they ate, they drank, they bought, they sold, they planted, they built, but on the day that Lot went out of Sodom it rained fire and brimstone from Heaven and destroyed them all. Even so will it be in the day when the Son of Man is revealed' (Luke 17:28-30, 2 Peter 2:7).

"The world is asleep in its sin. But when all the Babylonian systems fall, in which humanity trusts, all must choose once and for all – will they spend eternity in Heaven or Hell? The offer of salvation will feel real when the world around them is collapsing. And this age must collapse for the reign of Christ to begin, before the creation of a new earth and Heavens!"

"When will the end of days begin?" I queried.

"The Lord Jesus Christ warned of the signs of the end times," said the angel. "These things must take place to prepare for the apostasy of the Church, the revelation of Antichrist and the return of Jesus Christ. Look for these twenty signs, which are the beginning of the sorrows (Matthew 24:1-51, Luke 21:7-19).

1. "False prophets will propagate counterfeit beliefs, pointing to other messiahs or anointed ones.

2. "Erroneous religions will deceive multitudes.

3. "You will hear of wars and rumours of wars.

4. "Ethnic groups will rise against ethnic groups.
5. "Nation will rise again nation.
6. "There will be famines.
7. "Expect pestilences leading to pandemics.
8. "Earthquakes will shake nations.
9. "There will be fearful sights and signs from Heaven.
10. "Intolerance against Christians will rise.
11. "Christians will be killed for their faith worldwide.
12. "Hatred of Christian belief will rise from intolerance.
13. "People will be offended in an age of offence.
14. "Friends and family will betray one another.
15. "Spirituality will mislead many.
16. "Lawlessness will abound.
17. "The love of many will grow cold.
18. "The gospel will be preached in all the world.
19. "Many Christians will tire of waiting for Christ.
20. "Alcoholism and abuse will exist in churches.

"These twenty signs will change life on earth forever," explained the pitying angel. "Earthquakes, pestilences, tsunamis, hurricanes, famines and wars will break the sequence of normal life. Economies will crumble and infrastructure will break. Governments will shake and fall. This is just the beginning of the sorrows. However, the end will not come immediately" (Luke 21:9).

"This is just the beginning!" I said, in apprehension.

"People will not know where to seek for answers," said the angel. "During this shaking people should look to God for help. But many will turn to man, preparing the way for the Antichrist, just as the Great Depression paved the way for Hitler."

"Will this take place in a few years?" I asked.

"Presently, you are living in the Age of Slumber. People are content with all this life offers and have become blind to eternal reality. This is one reason why Paul said, 'Awake, you who sleep, arise from the dead and Christ will shine on you.'

"Mankind is in a spiritual slumber and is dead in sins. They have been rocked to sleep by the devil, as he keeps them mesmerised by all this life can offer. People are blinded to eternal realities by empty promises. They love entertainment and escapism (Romans 3:23,

Ephesians 2:2, 5:14, Colossians 2:13).

"I tell you a truth which few wish to hear. Satan has a keen interest in the prosperity of your nations. As they prosper, they turn from God in their hearts and reject His salvation; this is one lesson from Scripture. When prosperity came to Israel, the nation turned from serving the living God. It is the same today. People are fighting to keep temporal goods, whilst losing their eternal soul.

"The Lord warned His people through Jeremiah: 'I spoke to you in your prosperity, but you said, "I will not hear." This has been your manner from your youth, that you did not obey My voice.' Zechariah also warned God's people they stopped listening to Him when they are wealthy (Jeremiah 22:21, Zechariah 7:7).

"God's blessing of provision became blindness to those who love wealth more than the Lord. This demonic blindness kept the people of Noah's time ignorant of eternal realities. Just as the greatest disaster was about to break out, they were bewitched with their temporal lives. Think on the words of Jesus again, 'As it was in the days of Noah, so it will be also in the days of the Son of Man: They ate, they drank, they married wives, they were given in marriage, until the day that Noah entered the ark, and the flood came and destroyed them all' " (Luke 17:26-27).

"Everyone will be busy with their lives," I concluded.

"The Lord spoke of this spiritual blindness in the Parable of the Great Supper. People are bewitched in this world by all they think they want and need. In Jesus' parable, each person found an excuse to ignore God's call. One was busy buying a property, another had a business; another was lost in love, with plans for marriage and a family. They all lost sight of eternity (Luke 14:16-24).

"Mankind has been focusing on their short time on earth. Yet for the passing pleasure of a few decades, millions are losing their soul. It is not eighty years you will spend in Heaven or Hell, it is eternity! There is no end on the other side. This life is a test, to discover if you can be trusted with eternal riches" (Genesis 6:3, Psalm 90:10).

"Eternity is beyond us," I confessed.

"Does it matter if millions lose their prosperity for a short season to save their eternal soul? Can you not perceive the mercy of God? He is giving them a chance to receive eternal wealth, security and safety."

"There must be another way," I said.

"Your heart has been hardened to the mercy of God. You think it is unfair for God to judge the world in the Tribulation. Too many are dying in comfortable beds with no thought of eternity. They are just seconds away from Heaven or Hell and the devil wants them to slip away without a thought toward God.

"Millions in the West have been raised in a culture of rights and expectant prosperity. This has led to hardness of heart and the refusal to accept eternal realities. This will end!

"The Bible is the most honest book in the world. God allowed Job and many others to complain about the injustice they felt. Afterwards, the Lord confronted Job with reality and it silenced him. God always had something better planned for Job, as He does for all who repent during the end times. Their temporal suffering will lead to eternal joy (Job 40:3-5, 42:1-6, James 5:11).

"I tell you this, God is just. He will judge the world; He will right all wrongs. It is not His desire that anyone should perish and He takes no delight in the death of the wicked. In the last days, men will lose their temporal things, in order for them to gain the eternal. The new earth and Heavens will be joy indeed."

"Can humanity be saved without this suffering?" I inquired.

"Child of God, have you not understood? All civilisations come to an end. Every story has a beginning and an end. This world must end too. Think on the words of Jesus: 'O Jerusalem, Jerusalem, the one who kills the prophets and stones those who are sent to her. How often I wanted to gather your children together, as a hen gathers her brood under her wings, but you were not willing!' " (Luke 13:34).

I was shown a rubbish heap of goods and a scrapyard. I saw mountains of old clothes, gadgets, computers and vehicles. Everything the heart could imagine was heaped up in mountains of trash.

"Would you give your soul for this?" asked the angel.

"No," I said.

"But millions have. All you see was once someone's dream. Do you see what trash people give their lives for? People sacrificed their health, relationships, marriages and children for this. They claimed they were too busy for God because they wanted to own this rubbish. Let me open your eyes. Everything you buy is already in the process of decaying or becoming obsolete. This is the way of the world, decay has penetrated all things."

"We waste our lives on folly," I accepted.

"People lose their eternal soul for trash!" replied the angel. "Jesus said, 'For what will it profit a man if he gains the whole world and loses his soul? Or what will a man give in exchange for his soul?' Two thousand years have passed since the Lord asked these questions and people are still storing up mountains of trash on earth, and have not invested in eternal treasure" (Matthew 6:19-21, Mark 8:36-37).

"Consumerism is deception," I acknowledged.

"You live in the season of grace," explained the angel, "but it will end suddenly. This period of grace has lasted over two millennia; since the gospel was first preached and yet they still rebel. Experience has taught the greater the grace, the longer the rebellion. The time is soon upon all" (Isaiah 26:9-11).

Chapter Four

Israel, the Key to the End Times

I saw Jewish men praying at the Wailing Wall in Jerusalem and the angel said, "Israel – the key to the end times!"

"Bless the Jews in Jesus' name," I replied.

"There is coming a time when history will double back," said the angel. "Humanity will return to the follies of a previous age. I speak about the return of the Noah generation.

"In Noah's age, civilisation as man calls it, reached a grotesque level of corruption, so vast it passed the point of no return. In this time, humanity hardened its heart until it became as stone toward God. They shut their eyes and covered their ears, as they refused to heed the Lord's warnings, delivered by love. They mocked when they should have wept before God's altar. What followed this rebellion was mankind filling the earth with violence in their greed and the blood of the innocent cried out for justice" (Genesis 4:10, 6:13-7:24, 2 Kings 24:4, Psalm 9:12, Job 41:24, Ezekiel 36:26).

"Terrible," I said.

"People have taken the grace of God for granted today," said the angel. "They believe they've got away with sin. People think God does not exist because He does not strike them down. They mock the grace of God. The Almighty proclaims: 'Is it not because I held My peace from of old that you do not fear Me?' (Isaiah 57:11).

"As I have told you, Jeremiah spoke rightly when he declared, 'I spoke to you in your prosperity, but you said, "I will not hear." ' Therefore, heed the warning given to Ezekiel about the last generation: 'An end! The end has come upon the four corners of the land' (Ezekiel 7:2).

"There is coming a time when civilisation will once again harden its heart to such a grotesque state, that it goes beyond the possibility of repentance. It has already happened to many. The Lord offers them mercy through repentance, but they reject it in their pride (Genesis 18:20-19:26, Isaiah 34:1-17, Jeremiah 51:1-58, Ezekiel 7:1-27).

"Grace is flourishing in abundance, but mankind refuses to believe in grace or repentance. Those who seek to cancel God's plan will be cancelled themselves. 'We are not an evil age,' they say. And how has God replied in the past? 'Amos, what do you see?' So Amos said, 'A basket of summer fruit.' Then the Lord said, 'The end has come.' Have you not heeded the warnings given by the Holy Spirit to Peter? 'The end of all things is at hand!' " (Amos 8:2, 1 Peter 4:7).

"These are dark days for holiness," I conceded.

"As the men of Sodom were exceedingly wicked against the Lord, so is this generation. Their rebellion lays the foundation for the Rebel. The Antichrist is coming! He is the symbol of all rejection of God's will" (Genesis 13:13, 2 Thessalonians 2:3).

"What will be the character of the Antichrist?" I asked.

"The Antichrist will unveil his true self as he rises to power," said the angel. "He will appear to be what he is not. As he amasses power, he will show his true colours. Look out for these twenty signs of the Antichrist from Scripture: (Daniel 11:36-39).

1. "He will exalt himself.
2. "He will heed his inner voice above others.
3. "He will be hostile toward the true God.
4. "He will exalt human logic above faith.
5. "He will prosper for a season and be loved.
6. "He will not desire women.
7. "He will not follow the faith of his fathers.
8. "He will viciously persecute Jews and Christians.
9. "He will think of himself as greater than God.
10. "He will become increasingly lawless.
11. "He will honour military power above faith.
12. "He will love wealth.
13. "He will hoard precious things.
14. "He will become a man of war.
15. "He will wage a war on all people of faith.
16. "He will force Israel to sign a treaty.

17. "He will divide Israel and Jerusalem.

18. "He will invade Jerusalem.

19. "He will enter the restored Temple.

20. "He will declare himself above God.

"Yes, the Antichrist is coming. To prepare for his coming, little antichrists are creating a culture to welcome him."

"How can we get ready?" I asked.

"In churches, there will be false teachers who will worship conformity culture above Scripture. In the world, there will be leaders teaching rebellion against the Lord. Both are laying a foundation for the Antichrist. Their message will be peace and unity at all cost. When the truth costs or divides, they will reject it. They will worship a Jesus made in their image" (1 John 2:18-19).

"Lord, protect us from false teachers," I whispered, in prayer.

"There are also antichrist religions," said the angel. "These faiths compel men and women to reject Christ as their Saviour. Many put their faith in the teaching of a false prophet. John tells it well: 'Whoever denies the Son does not have the Father.' To know God the Father, you must accept Jesus the Son. All who claim to love God in the world, without Christ, are embracing the spirit of antichrist (John 14:6, 1 John 2:23).

"But there is another type of antichrist on earth. It is the antichrist system embedded into the culture and it's already established. From a young age, children are brought up in a civilisation that breeds rebellion toward Christ. They may call it progressive, woke or liberal; we call it antichrist (1 John 4:3).

"The antichrist culture paves the way for the total rejection of God's will. This will eventually lead to the person of the Antichrist (2 Thessalonians 2:3-4).

"There is an evil age ahead; a period when mankind's heart will be twisted by sin until they refuse to accept the possibility they have gone astray. This generation, deceived by its web of iniquity, will be enslaved by the spirit of wickedness. They will deceive themselves until the culture is beyond redemption. They will mock repentance because they cannot accept they've turned in the wrong direction. This is the lesson of Noah's age. It is the legacy of Sodom and Gomorrah."

"Help us," I pleaded.

"The antichrist culture has become so embedded into society, people do not even perceive it as antichrist. The evidence is everywhere. Almost every Christian principle and value are under attack."

"Christians will resist," I said.

"This antichrist system is tied to prosperity," said the angel. "As the sinner becomes wealthier, the deeper their sin becomes. This is called Babylon in Scripture. Unseen demonic powers will bring prosperity and 'bless' their wicked ways to damn souls" (Matthew 6:24, Ephesians 6:12, Revelation 18:23, 20:3).

"Wealth can be misleading," I accepted.

"These two satanic systems of power – the antichrist culture and the unseen powers of darkness will merge their strength, leading to the emergence of the Antichrist. Thus, when humans reject the truth of Christ, they open the door to embrace deception."

"Should we expect a sign in the sky to warn Christians of the end times?" I asked.

"Is the sign of a nation enough?" the angel asked.

"The greatest sign of the chosen nation reborn in a day has already taken place. The sign is Israel" (Isaiah 66:8).

"Of course," I acknowledged.

"Whilst countless numbers of nations, kingdoms and peoples have vanished from history, the people of Israel have remained a distinct ethnic and religious group. The Bible prophesied they would return to the land God gave them. You have taken the State of Israel for granted; remember in AD 70 the Temple in Jerusalem fell. After 1,800 years the Jews were still in exile. Many people gave up hope in the promises of Scripture. But those who believed witnessed Israel's rebirth 1,878 years after their exile" (Ezekiel 37:7-14).

"Why is Israel important in the end times?" I asked.

"The Spirit of Christ speaks concerning God's prophetic future for Israel in Scripture. Jesus already sits on the throne of David and He will sit on this throne in Jerusalem! The Antichrist wants this throne and will try to seize it (Matthew 24:15-16, Luke 1:32, 2 Thessalonians 2:4, 1 Peter 1:11, 1 John 2:22, 4:3).

"Israel is key because the Lord promised the land of Canaan to Abraham and his descendants forever, with no terms or conditions attached. God describes this covenant as everlasting. Do you understand what everlasting means?" (Genesis 17:7, 13, 19, 1 Chronicles 16:17, Psalm 105:10).

"Yes," I replied, "it means to continue indefinitely, forever. It has no end."

"Listen to Scripture: 'Thus says the Lord. If you can break My covenant with the day and My covenant with the night, so that there will not be day and night in their season, then My covenant may also be broken with David My servant, so that he shall not have a son to reign on his throne.' The throne of David is occupied by Jesus Christ forever" (Jeremiah 23:5, 28:16, 30:9, Isaiah 9:7, 11:1, Matthew 21:9, Luke 1:32, 69, Acts 13:34, Revelation 3:7).

"Jesus is the King of kings," I exclaimed.

"God made two unconditional covenants with Israel," he continued. "The first was with Abraham, the second with King David (1 Chronicles 17:11-14, 2 Chronicles 6:16).

"The Lord promised King David an unbreakable covenant. The Lord said, 'His seed also I will make to endure forever and his throne as the days of Heaven.' Jesus is in Heaven today sitting upon this throne, waiting to return to earth at the command of God the Father (2 Samuel 7:15-16, Psalm 89:29).

"The Scriptures also prophesied the Jews would reject their Messiah before it happened. This is why God planned ahead. Listen to these words: 'My covenant I will not break, nor alter the Word that has gone out of My lips. Once I have sworn by My holiness, I will not lie to David: His seed shall endure forever and his throne as the sun before Me; it shall be established forever like the moon, even like the faithful witness in the sky' (Psalm 89:30-37, 118:22).

"Even if the Jewish people want to revoke their covenant with God, they cannot! God has covenanted with Abraham their father and David, their first great King!

- 30 -

Those in the Church who teach the restoration of Israel in 1948 was a secular gathering are in error. The Church does not replace Israel (Romans 11:1-36).

"Even Isaiah foresaw this. God told him there would be two ingatherings to Israel. The first was a brief, partial return after the Babylonian captivity. The prophecy said a remnant would return. A few did return, but most of Israel was scattered in captivity and did not return (Ezra 2:64-67).

"The second gathering the prophet foresaw was a worldwide garnering and return of the Jews to Israel: 'It shall come to pass in that day that the Lord shall set His hand again the second time to recover the remnant of His people who are left, from Assyria and Egypt, from Pathros and Cush, from Elam and Shinar, from Hamath and the islands of the sea' (Isaiah 11:11).

"Isaiah foreknew the Jews would return to Israel from all over the world and from the four corners of the earth, the Jews have returned to Israel from more than one hundred nations. Countless other people groups have assimilated and been lost, but not the Jews! God kept them unique and has drawn them back to His land" (Isaiah 11:12).

"Hallelujah," I exclaimed.

"God has not been taken by surprise by their lack of faith in Jesus, the Christ," explained the angel. "Ezekiel prophesied Israel would return in unbelief: 'For I will take you from among the nations, gather you out of all countries and bring you into your own land. Then I will sprinkle clean water on you and you shall be clean; I will cleanse you from all your filthiness and from all your idols' (Ezekiel 36:24-25).

"First, God brings the Jews back to Israel in an unbelieving state and second He will restore them in His perfect timing. He brings them back in a position of idolatry as most worship self, money and the world. Then the Lord will restore them by sprinkling the clean water of the living Word in their hearts. Notice it is not a deluge to begin with, but one by one. He will open their hearts, little by little, as He sprinkles His living Word on them, until the day comes when the Lord reveals Himself as their

Messiah, King and Saviour.

"Paul put it like this: 'For what if some did not believe? Will their unbelief make the faithfulness of God without effect? Certainly not!' The new covenant with the Church stands side by side with the covenant God made with Abraham. God grafted the Church into the Vine and God is able to graft the Jews in again. Paul concluded: 'Concerning the election they are beloved for the sake of the fathers. For the gifts and the calling of God are irrevocable' (Romans 3:3-4, 11:23-29).

"Israel is the elect of God. Their calling is irrevocable. As God swore an everlasting covenant with Israel, He will keep it. No matter how good or bad they have been. God keeps all His promises and Israel will be restored. The Lord says of Israel, 'I will take the heart of stone out of your flesh and give you a heart of flesh' " (Ezekiel 36:25, Romans 11:1-32).

"What does this mean for the Jews in Israel?" I asked.

"For two thousand years, the Jewish people have had a heart of stone towards their Messiah. Centuries of persecution by alleged Christians solidified their rejection of Jesus Christ. But God can break down all barriers. The Spirit of God has sprinkled His Word into their heart. More Jews have been finding their Anointed One in this season, than since the days of the apostles. This is God's work and God's hour!"

"Will Christ return before or after the restoration of the Jews?" I asked.

"The return of Christ to the world has always been tied to the restoration of the Jews. Every biblical prophecy which relates to the close of this age predicts one unassailable factor – the presence of Israel, as a sovereign nation, within its own borders. The Church is not permitted to remain neutral or apathetic to God's revealed will for Israel. It is His will to keep them in their land and for their redemption.

"In the four Gospels you find Jesus Christ speaking as a Jew in Jerusalem, to the Jews of this holy city. When He spoke of the Temple he said, 'See! Your house is left to you desolate and assuredly, I say to you, you shall not see Me until the time comes when you say, "Blessed is

He who comes in the name of the Lord." ' He was speaking to the Jews as a collective people when Jesus said, 'You were not willing,' and 'Your House.' Thus, the Temple in Jerusalem was desolate within the lifetime of those who heard Christ (Luke 13:34-35, 19:41-44).

"This means Christ will not return until the Jews are ready to welcome Him! This is why the restoration of Israel is essential. First the physical restoration and second the sprinkling of the people. This leads to the opening of their heart, and finally, the Spirit of grace and supplication will be poured upon them. At this point, when Antichrist is reigning, they will acknowledge Jesus Christ as their Messiah, together as one nation" (Zechariah 12:10-14).

"There is so much hostility towards Israel in the media," I said.

"Satan knows when Christ returns his rule is finished," explained the angel. "He will be bound for one thousand years before his final destruction. As Satan cannot stop Christ from returning, he works in proxy. If he can destroy Israel, he thinks he can stop the fulfilment of prophecy. Thus, he seeks to find people he can work through to remove the Jews from the land. It begins with poisoning people's minds against the Jews and the State of Israel (Revelation 20:2, 7-10).

"Forget politics, it's a smokescreen. Satan is trying to stop Israel from being in the right place, at the right time, for her restoration and the return of Christ. This is the reason the antichrist spirit raised a false prophet to claim Jerusalem (1 John 2:22, 4:3, 2 John 7).

"The demonic spirit which possessed Haman possesses many today. Haman complained the Jews did not abide by their legal obligations. They make the same complaint today before a multitude at the United Nations. Through faith, Daniel and Esther bound the enemy in their day, but those principalities and powers never went away. They seek other willing vessels through whom their demonic power can be released to destroy Israel (Esther 3:8-9, Daniel 10:13-20, Ephesians 6:12).

"When Satan finds his vessels, he will think he is conquering, but it is Christ who is in charge. In the end time revelation given to John, he wept when no one was found worthy to open the scroll to usher in the last days. But One was found. A Jewish Messiah came forth from the seed of David. Listen to what the apostle heard: 'Do not weep. Behold, the Lion of the tribe of Judah, the Root of David, has prevailed to open the scroll and to loose its seven seals' (Revelation 5:5).

"Heaven did not find a Gentile to usher in the end times, but the One who sits on the throne of David. He is the Head of Judah, the King of Israel, the Anointed One, Jesus Christ" (Matthew 24:5, Luke 1:32).

"Amen," I said, with joy.

"The Messiah is coming for the Jews first," said the angel, "and Jesus was speaking of the Jewish people in many passages in the Gospels. The Gentile mind is not renewed and cannot discern when the Lord was speaking of the Jews. One warning Jesus gave was many false Messiahs would claim to be Him.

"In Jewish thought, there have been over forty significant people claiming to be the Anointed One or Messiah. The Jews did not expect a suffering servant, but a victorious king, ushering in a golden age of peace.

"In the second century, Simon bar Kokhba was the most prominent person who claimed to be the Anointed One to save the Jewish nation. One by one he began to meet the criteria Jewish thinkers pronounced for their messiah. He beat the Romans for a time and established an independent Jewish state. One of his goals was the building of the Third Temple and he made a start. In light of his success, Rabbi Akiva hailed him as their long awaited Messiah-King, ushering in the prophesied Messianic Age. But it all collapsed within three years."

"When will the Messiah-King come to Israel?" I asked.

"The Spirit of grace and supplication will be poured out upon Israel during the war of Armageddon and their spiritual eyes will be opened," explained the angel. "When they witness the resurrected Christ conquering their enemies, they will see the One they are looking for" (Zechariah 12:10-14).

Chapter Five

The Last Days Harbinger

The angel flew over Israel late at night crying out, "Israel, the sign of the last days." He came to rest at the height of the Mount of Olives' Jewish cemetery and I joined him.

The angel pointed his hands towards the Temple Mount and said, "The signs of the end times are all around, if you would only open your eyes!"

"Please tell me what these signs are," I said.

"There are six great end time signs concerning Israel," said the angel, "the harbinger of the end."

"The first is the restoration of the non-believing Jews to the land of Israel (Jeremiah 31:7-14, Ezekiel 36:16-38, Acts 1:6-7).

"The second is Jerusalem being restored as the capital of a sovereign Israel, which happened in 1967 (Zechariah 14:4, Luke 21:23-24).

"The third is the deserts blooming and the country exporting fruit to the nations. Isaiah said, 'Israel shall blossom and bud, and fill the face of the world with fruit' (Isaiah 27:6).

"The fourth is the birthing of a small remnant of Jews who acknowledge Jesus as their Messiah (Isaiah 10:20, Romans 11:5).

"The fifth is this remnant who believe in Jesus as their Messiah will grow and be blessed: 'For the seed shall be prosperous, the vine shall give its fruit, the ground shall give her increase and the Heavens shall give their dew – I will cause the remnant of this people to possess all these' (Zechariah 8:12).

"The sixth is the greatest of them, the restoration of the Jews who survive the Tribulation; they will recognise Jesus as their Messiah-King. He does not belong to the Church first, but to the Jews" (Matthew 15:24, Romans 1:16).

"Six great signs!" I observed.

"The first sign is being completed, the second and third have come to fruition, the fourth and fifth are being fulfilled and the sixth will take place soon: 'For Israel shall be saved by the Lord, with an everlasting salvation. They shall not be ashamed or disgraced forever and ever' (Isaiah 45:17).

"The Lord God said, 'For I will take you from among the nations, gather you out of all countries and bring you into your land...I will call for the grain and multiply it, and bring no famine upon you. And I will multiply the fruit of your trees and the increase of your fields, so that you need never again bear the reproach of famine among the nations...not for your sake do I do this (Ezekiel 36:24-32).

"On the 15 May 1948, God fulfilled His promise to return the Jewish people to the land of Israel, as an independent country. A nation was born in a day! When the Lord called His people to the home of promise, the truth which Jesus kept from the disciples was revealed (Isaiah 66:8-9, Jeremiah 23:7-8, Acts 1:6-7).

"In June 1967, another prophecy of Jesus concerning the end time State of Israel was fulfilled: 'And Jerusalem will be trampled by Gentiles until the times of the Gentiles are fulfilled.' The experts declared it would be impossible for Israel to re-take Jerusalem and keep it from Jordan, yet they fulfilled prophecy with God's strength (Luke 21:24).

"Imagine if an enemy occupied London or Washington for two thousand years and the inhabitants were scattered around the world by foreign powers, would they be restored? Israel is the only nation this has happened to!"

"It makes me wonder how many signs there are," I said.

"Israel is a great sign, but it is not the only sign. Daniel foresaw the last days would differ from all of history. He trumpeted an explosion of knowledge and mass travel (Daniel 12:4).

"Do you realise you have access to more information at the click of a button, than most of the governments of history combined? One connected device today contains access to more knowledge than all the peoples of the

Middle Ages and beyond!

"Have you ever considered the history of travel in England? Before trains and cars, the majority of people did not leave their community. But you have seen parts of the world which your grandfather did not even know existed. You are living in the information age and access to travel is easier than ever before.

"There are many other examples of the signs of the times. The Bible predicted a day when the whole world would witness events simultaneously. This is only possible because of the internet, satellites, streaming, TV, radio and social media (Matthew 24:30, Revelation 11:9).

"The Bible predicts the last days will be times of wars, rumours of wars, famines, pestilence and earthquakes. Jesus warned believers will experience a rising tide of intolerance. The Lord said, 'You will be hated by all for My name's sake.' This would have been unthinkable during the Christian golden age in your nation! But now Christians are harassed for believing in the simplest of biblical truths from Jesus – that marriage is a union between one man and one woman for life, and that God created people in His image male and female (Genesis 1:27, Matthew 24:4-14, Mark 10:7-9, Mark 13:13).

"The Bible predicts a one world government will arise and it will have dominion over the smallest of tribes to the largest nations. This would have been impossible before globalisation. But now the European Union (EU) proves nations can be coerced to give up sovereignty in the hope of prosperity. Today, the United Nations is forcing countries to closer terms and the shadow leaders of the economic world are putting their puppets in positions of power (Revelation 13:7-8).

"Satan has always planned to bring the nations together in unity against God. This is why the Lord confused ancient languages and scattered the peoples across the world at Babel. One reason was to subvert Satan's effort to unite the peoples in a global, anti-God kingdom, subjected to demonic power. God ordains nation states and divided the peoples to restrain Satan's kingdom on earth (Deuteronomy 17:14-17, Acts 17:26-27).

"However, the devil is working to bring people together into a false unity, to the detriment of all. He urges them to share sovereignty to unite them under his demonic power, with the Antichrist as his vessel. Satan lives in darkness and does not reveal himself without purpose. He lurks behind charismatic secular leaders, whom he will consecrate with a satanic anointing to bring Antichrist to his throne. But take courage, Satan cannot do anything without God allowing it" (Revelation 17:17).

"It's difficult to accept a people at liberty will give their sovereignty to others," I suggested.

"Europeans already have," replied the angel. "Their borders, laws, benefits, trading agreements and much more are subject to European supremacy. Europeans were told these agreements would make trading easier. Instead, they are dominated by a huge bureaucracy that interferes with every area of their lives, in ways most do not understand. Look at the data, most Europeans and the states of Europe are poorer now than they were twenty years ago. The European Union absorbs wealth created by entrepreneurs, waters down democratic consent, increases unaccountable bureaucracy, hinders job creation with red tape, and refuses to acknowledge Europe's long Christian heritage and its freedoms."

"Europe is one question, America another," I replied.

"Power is seized upon weakness," said the angel. "Think of the United States overwhelmed with debt, shaken by unprecedented earthquakes and losing its advantage over new powers. As America turns from God and chooses leaders with godless plans, the Lord's blessing and protection is removed. The U.S. can only weaken when new generations arise who do not know the Lord or seek His protection. The first generation of rebels is already voting against God's will; you have known a generation who loves the Lord in the U.S., it will not always be so. As with Israel, so with Britain, as with Britain, so with the United States.

"The Bible says, 'When all that generation had been gathered to their fathers, another generation arose after them who did not know the Lord, nor the work which He had done for Israel' " (Judges 2:10).

"The legacy of liberty must continue in their hearts," I said. "They have been warned in Scripture, the Mark of the Beast is coming" (Revelation 13:16-18).

"Hundreds of millions of people have already diminished their liberty for convenience," the angel divulged. "Millions have shared mountains of information about themselves with godless companies. Sinister technology has overtaken the law and commonsense.

"Billions of photos have been uploaded with GPS data attached. Social media has made it possible to track the mundane lives and movements of millions, and this information is being handed over freely!

"Governments already practice mass surveillance and they have unlimited private data held on mega computers. The greater the data, the greater the control!

"Think about money! Why does the enemy want a cashless society? Each bank transaction, credit card, online purchase or statement, allows shadow leaders to know what you buy, for whom, with what purpose and where you plan to go. Big Brother is now.

"If you combine all data sources on computers, everything you do is collated, quantified and stored. Your digital footprint reveals almost every aspect of your life. Even the trend of your thought life is revealed in your private search history!

"Think of the data flow from Britain's GCHQ, MI5, MI6, the United States' CIA, FBI and the Pentagon, and the combined knowledge of the 'Five Eyes' of the Anglophone world – the US, Britain, Australia, Canada and New Zealand. What would happen if their intelligence gathering powers fell into the hands of an Antichrist system?

"You are living in a time of constant and unprecedented monitoring apparatus, and Communist China is laying the foundation for a nation of absolute surveillance and control.

"Close to eight hundred million surveillance cameras are now watching the world and it's growing each day. This data feed will eliminate privacy. If anyone combines all this information with social media posts, searches online, views on streaming services, digital books read, internet pages visited, GPS feeds from cars and phones, medical records and government databases – it's the end of privacy!"

"Christians have been warned of a coming one world government," I said. "I don't think they will comply."

"Life is more fragile than you dare to acknowledge," said the angel. "It's easy to hold high principles when they cost you little. However, when your very existence is squeezed, the carnal nature will lust for compromise in its desire for survival.

"The Soviet Union forced people out of their churches and believers said never in America. However, millions were forbidden to leave their homes and stayed away from their churches during the coronavirus pandemic!

"In the West, you have organised a way of life which makes you oblivious to your frailty. When the oil pipes fail and the roads are quiet, when food runs out and the water supplies are cut, when the heating is permanently off, and the medication does not arrive – then people will find what compromises 'Christians' will make to survive.

"On that day, people will give thanks for the one world government. They will pray for the inspirational leader who kept people fed, watered, warm and medicated. They will flip their fears; just like Christian leaders in Germany did for Adolf Hitler, when his policies reversed the crisis of the Great Depression. Nazi Germany's economic miracle which began in 1933, is the primary reason churches backed Hitler – food, warmth and false hope.

"In the day an earthquake shakes the fault lines of the world, the ring of fire will tear the San Andreas Fault and with it the heart of America. In those dark days which follow, people with high ideals will kill strangers to get the last tin of food from a ransacked shop. When the necessities of life are squeezed to despair, the hungry will beg to join the Antichrist system!"

"God forbid," I gushed.

"You do not know how vulnerable your civilisation is," explained the angel. "How will your businesses, planes, cars, phones, drones and food services work if every computer fails? How many have been born who have never read a map? How will traffic signals or communication systems work? How will electric cars move when there is no electricity? What happens when utilities fail? How will trade continue when container ships cannot navigate channels without computers? How will wars play out when high-end planes cannot fly without a computer operating in the background?

"Gold once defined the value of a currency. Today it's pixels on a computer screen. What happens when the screens won't turn on? How will you buy and sell? How will you live?

"You have government agencies designed to cope with one crisis at a time. What happens when ten take place at once? How many days did it take for a powerful nation – the richest on the planet – to get water to people trapped in New Orleans in 2004?

"Anything is possible as the Scriptures warn: 'Take heed to yourselves, lest your hearts be weighed down with carousing, drunkenness, and the cares of this life and that Day come on you unexpectedly. For it will come as a snare on all those who dwell on the face of the whole earth. Watch therefore and pray always that you may be counted worthy to escape all these things that will come to pass, and to stand before the Son of Man' " (Luke 21:3-36).

Chapter Six

The Prosperous Apostate Church

I saw churches gathering in different parts of the world. In the West, celebrations took place. There was a church that looked like a shopping mall. Everything you could imagine could be purchased or consumed in this mall of faith. When the church service began, people celebrated and the service felt like a party. Smoke machines blasted, lights and lasers flashed, and the worship team danced before the Lord.

The preacher was inspirational, and he filled his message with aggressive self-promotion and personal ambition. Young people wanted to be like him because he was trendy, muscular, tanned, wealthy and powerful in speech. The humble Jesus of the Gospels felt far from his sermons, as he advocated that believers can have everything this world possesses, whilst giving his sermons a veneer of spiritual truth.

"If you took away the smoke machine, the coffee bar and gym, do you think they would still come?" asked the angel. "Do you see a man crucified with Christ preaching, or a reflection of the aspirations of this fallen world?"

"He's doing what he can to reach people for Christ," I replied. "I know it's not a great reflection of discipleship, but he's trying."

After speaking, I saw an underground church meeting in a home in the Middle East, worshipping silently. They were praying with tears, asking the Lord for a pure heart and seeking strength to remain faithful. In the spiritual realm angels surrounded them and stood by witnessing their perseverance. One by one they left the home to avoid people noticing the gathering.

"Which church do you believe has purity of heart?" asked the angel.

"You know the answer," I replied.

"Think on these things," he said. "Knowledge of the end

times is of no importance, unless you heed the command to repent. You must become like little children. All must repent in humility and get ready for the coming Lord. Days of darkness are converging upon the world and the Lord will return for a holy Church."

"Help us," I sighed.

"The admonishing of Jesus to the seven churches in the Book of Revelation contains signs for each generation. Learn from the sin and goodness of the churches!"

"What are the lessons we must learn?" I asked.

"To five of the churches Jesus said, "I know your works," and He commanded them to repent. This means most Christians worldwide – over seventy percent by this calculation – must repent. This includes you!

"The trials of the persecuted and persevering churches keep them untainted because persecution brings purity. They must hold fast and not give in to temptation."

"God help them," I said.

"May the Lord help Christians deceived by prosperity," replied the angel. "You should pray daily, 'Lord, keep us from deception.' Listen to me: Christians must repent, hold fast and be faithful."

"I am listening," I declared.

"The first church in the Book of Revelation lost its love for Christ," explained the angel. "This is the church where religious observance becomes more important than following Jesus and heeding His Spirit. They do many things but do not sit at the feet of the Master (Luke 10:38-41, Revelation 2:1-7).

"The second is the suffering church. The Lord praises it and encourages it to continue in the faith. The Lord will help them, but they will face prison and martyrdom (Revelation 2:8-11).

"The third is the worldly compromised church. This is the church that follows the ways of popular culture. The love of money and spiritual idolatry taints it. This church seeks power by witchcraft and falls into sexual perversion. Greed, with excessive preaching about wealth is unacknowledged idolatry (Colossians 3:5, 2 Peter 2:15, Jude 1:11, Revelation 2:14-16).

"The fourth church is manipulated by the spirit of

Jezebel. A demonic female prophet that dominates men seduces this congregation. It seeks to serve God, but sins by falling into idolatry and sexual immorality. Those who refuse to repent for following Jezebel will not escape the Tribulation (1 Kings 18:4-21:25, 2 Kings 9:10-37, Revelation 2:20-23).

"The fifth church is traditional and soiled by worldliness. This is a congregation founded by an illustrious name in each generation in blood and fire. But it is now dead. Its leaders spend more time managing decline and closing church buildings than saving souls (Revelation 3:1-6).

"The sixth church is persevering. This is the church filled with people willing to go through the open door God has for them. They move forward regardless of opposition, their strength has been tested, but they are faithful to God's Word and will not renounce Jesus for the world. Their faithfulness will protect them from the coming Tribulation (Revelation 3:7-13).

"The seventh church is lukewarm. This is the church that thinks wealth is a sign of God's favour. They think they have no need for anything because they have plenty of money. They do not know their obsession with temporal things is spiritual immaturity. They are wretched, miserable, poor, blind and naked in the spiritual realm. They are children playing in the mud thinking they have found true wealth. This church is rebuked because God loves them. Only repentance can restore spiritual wealth. The Lord wants them to seek eternal value and be refined in the fire, to be clothed with spiritual maturity" (Revelation 3:14-22).

"The persecuted Church in China is growing," I said. "But the problem of lukewarmness is persistent in the West."

"There are men preaching messages which are not from God," said the angel. "They have become accustomed to the praise and applause of people. Their sermons are twisted to please listeners. Paul warned of this saying, 'Let no one deceive you by any means; for that Day – the return of Christ – will not come unless the falling away comes first' (John 12:43, 2 Thessalonians 2:3).

"Paul was not the only one to warn you. John foretold

these days saying, 'Beloved, do not believe every spirit, but test the spirits, whether they are of God; because many false prophets have gone out into the world. By this you know the Spirit of God: Every spirit that confesses Jesus Christ has come in the flesh is of God, and every spirit that does not confess that Jesus Christ has come in the flesh is not of God. And this is the spirit of the antichrist, which you have heard was coming, and is now already in the world. You are of God, little children and have overcome them, because He who is in you is greater than he who is in the world' " (1 John 4:1-4).

"I wonder how many Christians are deceived," I contemplated.

"The worst form of deception is religious fraudulence. There are preachers who twist God's Word for personal financial gain; they are slaves to deceiving spirits and preach the doctrines of demons" (1 Timothy 4:1).

"I wonder which preachers are teaching the doctrines of demons today," I pondered.

"Jesus said you will know them by their fruits. Remember, it is not the words of people you must listen to; you should watch the fruit of their lives. The wisest devil speaks through smiling faces. Those seated on golden thrones of prosperity esteem their comfort above the horror of those dying without Christ (Matthew 7:16-20, 2 Corinthians 11:14).

"The Bible says: 'But know this, that in the last days perilous times will come: For men will be lovers of themselves, lovers of money, boasters, proud, blasphemers, disobedient to parents, unthankful, unholy, unloving, unforgiving, slanderers, without self-control, brutal, despisers of good, traitors, headstrong, haughty, lovers of pleasure rather than lovers of God, having a form of godliness but denying its power. And from such people turn away!' (2 Timothy 3:1-5).

"The great warning from Scripture is these people have 'a form of godliness.' They are religious people with the 'acceptable' sins of being lovers of self, greedy for money and proud of their knowledge of the Bible! They are lovers of pleasure, not God. The last thing on their mind is the teaching of Jesus: 'If anyone desires to come after

Me, let him deny himself, and take up his cross daily and follow Me' " (Luke 9:23).

"There is a true and false Church," I asserted.

"When Satan introduces a simple right or wrong choice, it compels Christians to ingest truth and choose," said the angel. "But when Satan tempts believers to make a systematic set of small, seemingly insignificant compromises, they will follow him; even if it leads to alienation from God!

"These false teachers do not live for the next world; nor do they sacrifice to hasten the coming of the reign of Christ, because they are busy trying to reign now (2 Peter 3:12).

"They raise champions, prophesy all will be rich and distort the heart of the gospel. They desire the wealth and influence of Caesar, rather than the riches found with the crucified Christ (Matthew 11:8-10, Luke 16:13).

"They elevate self instead of dying to it. In place of loving sacrificially, they teach selfishness and call it faith. Some bring in destructive heresies, even denying the Lord, whilst others exploit the hearer with deceptive words for dishonest gain (1 Corinthians 15:31, 2 Peter 2:1-3, 3 John 2).

"They have enough of God's Word to make it feel plausible, with plastic smiles, false humility and best-selling books on self-elevation. They want to meet with presidents but not the poor, unless it's for a photo opportunity. They would fall immediately under persecution (Matthew 6:3-4).

"The Corinthians were warned of said preachers: 'For if he who comes preaches another Jesus whom we have not preached, or if you receive a different spirit which you have not received, or a different gospel which you have not accepted – you may well put up with it!' (2 Corinthians 11:4).

"If you listen with a true heart, with the gift of discernment from the Holy Spirit, you will learn the only thing they are promoting is themselves. Like dragons in stories, they sit on a mountain of wealth, sent to them by desperate souls hoping for a miracle. These false teachers have walked down the path of self-deception for so long, they believe they are serving God. They reject the message of the true prophets and heap up for themselves false prophets to preach what they want to hear (Jeremiah 6:14, 8:11, Ezekiel 13:10, 13:16, Luke 13:34, John 16:2).

"They want all to come up higher, but Christ wants you to humble yourself. They want to raise champions, but Christ wants servants. They want all to be rich now but Christ desires treasure in Heaven. They urge you to prove your spiritual depth by possessing mountains of goods. But the Lord teaches you can only keep what you give away" (Matthew 6:20, Mark 10:21, Luke 9:23-25, John 13:12-17, James 4:10).

"When they quote the Bible, it can be hard to distinguish what is false and true," I replied.

"These famous speakers possess everything the flesh desires and sprinkle it with the illusion of spiritual prestige. But, if a preacher never speaks of exposing sin, purging repentance and sacrificial faith in Christ's shed blood, you should be concerned. Those who belong to God will preach a crucified life in Christ (Galatians 2:20).

"God's preachers will declare you must surrender yourselves entirely to Him. They will tell you to live with eternity in mind, to follow the example of Christ and His apostles. If the lifestyle of the preacher you're listening to is at odds with the example of Jesus, beware" (Matthew 12:36-42, Luke 16:1-31, Luke 21:3-37, John 10:27-28, Romans 12:1-2, Colossians 3:2-4).

"Jesus said to His disciples, 'If anyone desires to come after Me, let him deny himself and take up his cross, and follow Me. For whoever desires to save his life will lose it, but whoever loses his life for My sake will find it. For what profit is it to a man if he gains the whole world and loses his soul? Or what will a man give in exchange for his soul?' " (Matthew 16:24-26).

"Perhaps in the end times many Christians will choose comfort over truth," I accepted.

"The compromises needed to accept the Antichrist and a world government have already been made by millions in their churches," the angel explained.

"Esau was the firstborn who sold his birthright for a bowl

of food. He sold his legacy; his past, future and the call of God for one meal. People do not quote the God of Abraham, Isaac and Esau because he chose ease over the call. In the last days, many Christians will sell out like Esau and give everything away for the temporal (Genesis 25:29-34, Hebrews 12:14-17).

"When Satan came against the early Church, his attacks were straightforward and blunt. He tried to get the authorities to force people to renounce Jesus Christ and stop preaching. This strategy failed because when Christians are given a black and white choice, they are forced to come to terms with what they truly value. Thus, many Christians were prepared to die for their faith for centuries. They concluded it's better to be martyred and be rewarded in paradise, than compromise with sin (Acts 4:17-22).

"Roman believers discovered if you have found nothing worth dying for, you have found nothing worth living for! Thus, facing defeat as the Church grew under persecution, Satan changed his strategy. He decided to rock the Church to sleep with ease. He found preachers to help him (Amos 6:1, 1 John 4:5).

"Peter warned false teachers will exploit covetousness – your lusts for wealth, power, influence and prestige: 'But there were also false prophets among the people, even as there will be false teachers among you, who will secretly bring in destructive heresies, even denying the Lord who bought them and bring on themselves swift destruction. And many will follow their destructive ways, because of whom the way of truth will be blasphemed. By covetousness they will exploit you with deceptive words; for a long time their judgment has not been idle and their destruction does not slumber' (2 Peter 2:1-3).

"If people can't resist the Apostate Church, they will struggle to perceive the Mark of the Beast when it arrives," said the angel. "When barcodes and credit cards with electronic chips were released, many Christian leaders feared it was a preparation for the Mark of the Beast, and they were right" (Revelation 13:17).

Chapter Seven

A Great Global Awakening

"The Apostate Church makes me wonder if everything in the end times is bad news," I said, with shrugged shoulders.

"The Bible accurately foretells the state of the Church before the Tribulation and the return of Christ," the angel said. "The love of many will grow cold and many hearts will be hardened. Don't forget Jesus asked a very pointed question: 'When the Son of Man comes, will He really find faith on the earth?' (Luke 18:8).

"In unbelief, many Christians have greater belief in the world's power to destroy faith, than in the power of God to redeem souls in revival power! They find it easier to accept doom and gloom, than believe in the promises of God for salvation! The enemy has got inside the minds of some Christians and is speaking through their pulpits, books, streaming services, social media and blogs."

"What should I avoid?" I asked.

"Beware of Christians who vomit doubt and unbelief, and call it discernment and wisdom," he replied.

"I have heard preachers say things will only get worse and there is no promise for revival in the Bible for our time," I replied.

"What Bible did the great revivalists of yesterday have?" the angel asked. "Jonathan Edwards, John Wesley, Evan Roberts, D.L. Moody and Duncan Campbell all claimed promises from the Bible for a Heaven-sent spiritual awakening. They accessed the same promises of God which you have to believe for revival. God's Word has not changed! God's promises are not revoked. If anything has changed, it's your heart – from faith to unbelief. Is anything too hard for the Lord?"

"No," I replied, "of course not."

"God has promised He will pour out His Spirit 'on all flesh' and it remains to be fulfilled. All those great revivals of history were a foretaste of what God promised He will do in Scripture, in the end times!"

"If God moves, many will be saved," I said.

"I tell you a secret which few can accept. The first to resist what God is doing will be religious Christians! Many in churches have already prepared their heart to reject what God is going to do. Before the global awakening of the Holy Spirit begins, they will reject the move because it's different from what they read about in history. They have made an idol of past awakenings, whilst rejecting what God is doing now. They have followed in the same unbelief of the Pharisees" (Luke 7:30).

"Should we then expect a global spiritual awakening before the Tribulation period?" I asked.

"As I have explained, the Word of God contains a promise which has yet to be fulfilled," said the angel. "The outpouring of God's Holy Spirit on a worldwide scale is prophesied in Scripture. It is absolutely clear in Joel's prophecy that the end time outpouring of the Holy Spirit is interlinked with the last days. Listen to Joel's vision: "And it shall come to pass afterward, that I will pour out My Spirit on all flesh. Your sons and your daughters shall prophesy, your old men shall dream dreams, your young men shall see visions. And also on My menservants and My maidservants, I will pour out My Spirit in those days. And I will show wonders in the Heavens and in the earth: Blood and fire and pillars of smoke. The sun shall be turned into darkness, and the moon into blood, before the coming of the great and awesome Day of the Lord. And it shall come to pass, that whoever calls on the name of the Lord shall be saved" (Joel 2:28-32).

"Amen," I rejoiced.

"The Holy Spirit will move worldwide in power," explained the angel. "Churches must prepare their hearts to be ready. Will you welcome or reject Him because He offends your religious spirit?"

"This revival is long coming," I confessed, "many have prayed."

"When you visited Heaven, you heard why revival tarries. The Church has not met the conditions of the four great 'ifs' of revival. You know the promise:

"If My people will humble themselves...

"If My people will pray...

"If My people will seek My face...

"If My people will turn from their wicked ways...

"Then God will hear from Heaven, and will forgive their sin and heal their land (2 Chronicles 7:14).

"The conditions have not been met, as you know. There have been many prayer meetings, but few willing to humble themselves in the dust before God. Many have stood on platforms to weep before large crowds, but few seek God's face on their own (Matthew 6:5).

"But I have good news also. The Lord found people to believe before, He will find them again! A generation will experience the outpouring of the Holy Spirit in a great awakening to prepare for Jesus' return. It has been delayed by disobedience, but it has not been cancelled. Nothing can stop God's plan!

"Today, there are many loveless churches estranged from the Lord (Revelation 2:1-7).

"Many persecuted churches in places such as China, parts of Asia, North Africa and the Middle East (Revelation 2:8-11).

"There are many compromised churches (Revelation 2:12-17).

"Corrupted churches (Revelation 2:18-29).

"Dead churches (Revelation 3:1-6).

"Struggling churches (Revelation 3:7-13).

"And lukewarm churches (Revelation 3:14-22).

"In all this, God has a faithful remnant; as with Israel, so with the Church (Matthew 25:1-14, Romans 9:27, 11:5).

"The last words of Jesus to His Church are recorded in the Book of Revelation. He did not speak to them about their wealth, happiness or temporal provisions, but to prepare for eternity. He told them to hold fast and repent.

"Jesus said, 'Behold, I am coming quickly and My reward is with Me, to give to every one according to his work. I am the Alpha and the Omega, the Beginning and the End, the First and the Last. I, Jesus, have sent My angel to testify to you these things in the churches. I am the Root and the Offspring of David, the Bright and Morning Star" (Revelation 22:12-13, 16).

Chapter Eight

666 – The Mark of the Beast

I entered a room covered with computers, each with code running down their screens. The heat was intense and cooling fans conveyed at high speed.

"Do you know what you see?" asked the angel.

"Computers," I said.

"It is your life," said the angel. "Everywhere you go, everything you share digitally, all you buy and every one you share it with."

"Big Brother," I said.

"666," replied the angel.

"How?" I asked.

"In the past, the British Empire and its successor, the United States, projected power with a carrot and stick approach. They deemed it cheaper to gain influence by giving aid, rather than fight wars. But in the last days, nations will come together into regional and then centralised unions. The legality of this shared sovereignty will become opaque; it will be impenetrable for the majority. They will not understand their liberty has been given away. This is the case with the European Union."

"How will it work?" I asked.

"The Bible predicts a time of earthquakes, floods, raging seas and many natural disasters. This will compel global leaders to work together. Forced cooperation is what made the Roman Empire possible (Matthew 24:3-44).

"Each crisis in the world will affect the world's economy. Bank collapses, debt crises, deficits and inflation will make printed money worthless. This is why a digital system will be required. Your money will just be pixels on a screen. When physical cash becomes limited, the powers can establish the Mark of the Beast as the only payment method."

"Will it be a chip implanted on the right hand or forehead?" I asked. "It could be embedded into human skin and integrated into individual DNA. Perhaps it could be synced to the unique electrocardiogram of each person's heartbeat!"

"The method is not the issue but the purpose," said the angel. "Think about it again! A system that connects all the data flows from one's life: An individual's bank account, social security number, medical data, and all private codes, integrated with shopping habits, internet searches and GPS location. All the geolocation and time information coming from your phone, car, computer, smart devices, combined with CCTV feeds, bank cards, store cards and purchases. There will be no privacy, freedom or rights. It's all the data which exists about you in one place!"

"The Church must resist," I said.

"False teachers will preach Christians should integrate saying, 'Rulers are not a terror to good works, but to evil.' But they will be blinded by the technology which 'causes all, both small and great, rich and poor, free and slave, to receive a mark on their right hand or on their foreheads, and that no one may buy or sell except one who has the mark or the name of the Beast, or the number of his name" (Romans 13:3, Revelation 13:16-17).

"I wonder how deep the mass surveillance already goes," I replied.

"As we have discussed already, governments have access to monitor your life and every life beyond your comprehension. They search and record everything they can, everywhere. They are swamped with information and for this reason they struggle to find a needle in the haystack. The intrusive surveillance goes beyond your appreciation. Smart devices and apps track and trace your life, and some secretly record your voice, advertising the thing you spoke about when you thought you were offline!"

"The data is there, but the system to sift it is not ready," I replied.

"Private companies hold data on everything you search and buy," he said. "They read your texts and emails, and know who you contact and socialise with, using social media and phone pings to find your location. They collect all your images with GPS tags, and track how long you spend looking at images and what buttons you click. They know what digital books you read and highlight. They document what posts you like, share and subscribe to. Health apps know more about your body than you. Think on this again! All health and lifestyle devices are collecting data. They know the real you. Zero privacy hour is now! The world has volunteered to surrender freedom!"

"Our lives are not that interesting," I said, hesitating, "who will use this against me? Not a democracy!"

"How quickly a democracy falls," replied the angel. "The world already possesses the tools to create a total surveillance society. China already has. All your gadgets are capable of recording, transferring and uploading data to a singular database. All these feeds can be translated into strings of computer code of zeros and ones capable of being searched, analysed, stored and hacked. Networked cars and smartphones give precise location data, providing a map of your whereabouts and journeys.

"The first generation which can be tracked from birth to death, with online storage backups of pictures, videos, locations, friendships, family, interests, jobs and faith affiliation is alive. Your digital footprint knows more about you than you!"

"It's unbelievable," I commented.

"That's just the official data collections. Think of the hackers, the viruses and the keyloggers. Consider hidden spying programs accessing information, following the keys struck on your keyboard, noting all you type. Hackers can log and store all emails, phone calls, texts, apps and online activity. Even your cameras and microphones can be turned on without consent. In the digital world anonymity is impossible."

"It's not good," I said.

"The Mark of the Beast is no longer a technical impossibility! You are living with the technology which the Bible predicted. If all the services and data providers were merged into one data collection source, the Mark of 666 would be with you – if it is not already!"

Chapter Nine

The Desire for a World President

In the spiritual realm, I walked through the streets of a devastated European city. For as far as the eye could see, once proud buildings were now reduced to piles of concrete slabs, rubble and twisted beams. Small fires smouldered in the ruins, and the principle boulevard was reduced to a pathway winding through shattered heaps of brick, steel and concrete. On both sides, steps led up towards the shells of homes and businesses.

A defunct newspaper blew through the ruins which simply read 'Earthquake' and contained an order for residents to evacuate, because the aftershocks increased in intensity. On the following pages, there were stories of ethnic conflict, wars, food shortages and the blockage of major shipping lanes. The journalists decried their leaders for failing to unify and work with other nations, to alleviate the impending crises distressing humanity.

Twenty years passed and a gathering of world leaders herded together to receive an address from the German Chancellor. She was popular and counted Angela Merkel as an inspiration from what she called, "A lost golden age." She was speaking from Berlin where the ancient 'Seat of Satan' resides in the Pergamon Museum. It went on display in 1930, as the antichrist spirit possessed a type in Hitler on his rise to power (Revelation 2:12).

"Only twenty years ago, the prospect of a union of multi-continental nations, working closely together within regional hubs was considered impossible," she said. "Yet, in the last two decades, most nations have come into agreement to establish our common cause.

"We are one small planet, fragile, unique and blessed. As we put aside our differences, we have founded a groundbreaking Global Union of the Ten Great Unions of earth, birthed out of the lessons of the European Union

(Daniel 7:7, Revelation 17:12).

"In each Union, unique sovereign nations have agreed to work together with unprecedented economic integration. This has established greater peace and stability. We are many nations, languages and cultures, and yet we are united in one peaceful Union to share in our common humanity."

To my surprise I heard jeers in the auditorium.

"This is a Union born out of necessity," she continued. "The chaos of the last few decades has cost us all. The Sino-West War was a bitter mistake. It left us unprepared for the crises ahead. When natural disasters hit Africa, food supplies in Europe were shaken. When floods crushed China, factories in South America went without supplies; our lives are interwoven.

"We must put the ethnic wars and strife of recent times in the past. Your problems are our problems. No longer are there rich and poor nations. We are one Union with universal problems, needing meaningful coordination.

"In every family of nations there will be disputes, but now all nations are working as one. Together we engage in dialogue instead of war. As one, we can build a shared future. I promise we can achieve more together than apart. We have more in common which unites us than divides.

"I know some nations feel forgotten. We the leaders of our countries are busy with the problems of our nations. We spend our time thinking about our domestic needs. When we do this, we lose the vision of what this Union can achieve. This is why we need a greater Union to solve international problems.

"For this reason, I propose we consider choosing a President of our World Union. One who can invest his or her time solely in the world's problems. We need the Winston Churchill or Abraham Lincoln of our age. One who sees past self-interest and can teach us another's problems are our own. If such an individual was chosen, all their energy could be directed towards the concerns of smaller nations."

There was cheering and loud applause.

"Events have taken hold quickly," said the angel. "In a

few decades since the beginning of this global crisis, the peoples of the world have joined in a worldwide system of governance. In each country, the resemblance of their former way of governance – be that democracy or dictatorship continues – as long as they sign up to the 'Vision' of the Union. By doing so every nation must be subject to the greater power of the Global Union.

"The Antichrist is quietly at work building a reputation and the nations recognise the need for one powerful decision-maker. But he is yet to arise. Shared sovereignty is the path: this happened with the EU, as European nations handed over their powers, without their citizens understanding it."

"Can this really happen to all?" I asked.

"Do you remember what I taught you before?" the angel replied. "People will give away their liberty in a heartbeat, when there's no water coming through the pipes, or food on the shelves. The Israelites rejoiced at the miracle of the Red Sea, but cried bitterly in hunger and thirst. Soon, they were making a golden idol and planned to return to Egyptian enslavement for the promise of food and water (Exodus 15:2-25, 17:1-3, 32:2-4, Numbers 11:4-6).

"It will be the same in the Last Days; nations will hand over power to a greater Union. They will do so, as long as they get to keep the resemblance of sovereignty. Each nation will have its own leader, but real power will exist elsewhere.

"Think of Greece. When this nation joined the Euro, they handed over 'paperwork' sovereignty in the eyes of the people. Things became better for a season. Few citizens believed their own liberty was at risk. Yet within a few short years, their entire economy was controlled by unnamed bureaucrats sitting in European Offices.

"The Bible says, 'Authority was given him over every tribe, tongue and nation.' This can only be fulfilled by a global Union of powers and the EU proves this can occur. The mere appearance of sovereignty is all that matters. In the European Union, local governments come and go, but the EU and its plans remain" (Revelation 13:7).

Chapter Ten

Preparation for Global Government

I began to see images of political buildings from the European Parliament to the headquarters of the United Nations. The angel told me of their significance to prepare for the Antichrist system.

"In your time there are bureaucrats, politicians, celebrities and business leaders – the shadow leaders of the world – pulling the strings of power towards planetary hegemony," he said. "Their goal is to create a world where all power resides with the global elite. In this shadow democracy, there will be a direction the world is heading which cannot be stopped by an election.

"The European Union and the United Nations are examples. They create unassailable hydra-headed agencies to deploy power regardless of the will of the people. Together they have usurped power from once sovereign nation states, accumulating it by stealth and attrition, concentrating it into the hands of few.

"Powerful shadow influencers are seeking to discredit the nation state to establish a one world government. They encourage collective mindsets, as individual liberty is being submerged, handing power to bureaucrats with a Big Brother mentality. The world is moving together:

1. "The United States is currently the world's greatest power, but many woke liberal leaders want to reject the values which made the nation strong, submitting to international institutions and the example of the EU.

2. "The Association of Southeast Asian Nations (ASEAN) of ten countries is rising.

3. "The African Continental Free Trade Agreement (AfCFTA) of twenty-eight nations is bringing Africa together, alongside the African Union.

4. "The Comprehensive and Progressive Agreement for Trans-Pacific Partnership (CPTPP) of eleven nations is developing.

5. "The Andean Community (CAN) of four South American nations is paving the way for greater cooperation in the region.

6. "The desire for the Middle East Free Trade Area (MEFTA) is developing.

7. "Shia and Sunni Muslim nations are aligning themselves to strengthen their position, creating structures of influence.

8. "The 85 federal subjects of the Russian Federation dominate vast areas in Europe towards Asia.

9. "Many of the official 55 ethnic groups inside the Empire of China feel they live under occupation by the Han Chinese. The symbol of China's boundary, the Great Wall of China, can be found 2000km away from China's present border! These peoples include the Zhuang, Hui, Manchu, Uyghur, Miao, Yi, Tujia, Tibetan, Mongol, Dong, Buyei, Yao, Bai, Hani, Li, Kazakh and Dai ethnic groups. But there are also hundreds of other ethnic groups in China that are unacknowledged by their government.

10. "The European Union is a forerunner to a global union, but don't put your trust in its stability."

"What can we learn from the EU?" I asked.

"The EU is far ahead in demeaning the power of the state to produce a super-state with the Euro, the currency of nineteen European nations. Europe's Single Market has twenty-seven nations and five non-EU states.

"The Euro is a forerunner to a world currency. World leaders and economic experts are already thinking of a supranational reserve currency. This would be a single world currency or super currency, with all powers submerged into the one supreme reserve. The elite are already talking about a global central bank.

"Heed the signs. The rise of digital global currencies provides a wider format for their plans. The clandestine leaders are already talking about a new international reserve asset. It's a form of the Special Drawing Rights (SDRs) of the International Monetary Fund (IMF). The major currencies of the U.S. dollar, the Euro, Pound Sterling, the Chinese and Japanese Yuan would back it, with the Russian Ruble, to establish a world currency."

"This is shocking," I said.

"Great Britain was the nation which stood alone against Nazi Germany in 1940 and it stood alone again with Brexit. As a member of the EU it restrained the growing integration, but when Britons voted to leave, the EU was weakened."

"What's the significance of the EU in the end times?" I asked.

"The Treaty on the Functioning of the European Union (TFEU), formerly known as the Treaty of Rome, was first signed in 1957 on Capitoline Hill, Rome," replied the angel.

"Listen to what John said of the Whore of Babylon: 'Here is the mind which has wisdom: The seven heads are seven mountains on which the woman sits.' The Seven Hills of Rome are Aventine, Caelian, Capitoline, Esquiline, Palatine, Quirinal and Viminal (Revelation 17:9).

"It was on one of these hills, Capitoline, where six heads of European governments put their signatures to a literal blank document in 1957. The text of the treaty was missing! Check your history. This signals in the spiritual realm that those who signed this treaty would lose control over the process. They gave away their sovereignty to an unknown spiritual power.

"Few realise the European leaders who signed this treaty held these blank pages, with a front cover and a page for the signatures. To the natural man, problems with time and printers led to this error. To the spiritual man, the leaders of Europe signed a blank treaty, giving their power away to an unknown future sinister source.

"But beware, the EU is not all you think it is. Times and seasons change. Empires come and go. In its present form it is a warning, a foreshadowing and the prophetic symbolism is clear.

"Strasbourg's EU Parliament building was designed with Bruegel's *Tower of Babel* as the template. It held the promise of 'Europe, many tongues, one voice.' It presents a fraudulent promise of democratic consent and is a rebellion against the judgment on Babel. They concentrate actual power in a tiny number of unelected elites of politicians and bureaucrats. Britons understood this and chose Brexit, freeing Britain from the EU.

"Outside of the European Council Building in Brussels, there is a statue of a woman riding a Beast. This image is also found on the two Euro coin. John warned: 'I will tell you the mystery of the woman and of the Beast that carries her, which has the seven heads and the ten horns' (Revelation 17:7).

"The EU has become fat by gorging on democracy. It eats away the rights and freedoms of its citizens. It resides on the ashes of the Roman Empire. The elite of the EU are getting richer, whilst European citizens are becoming poorer by the year.

"The EU, like the former Roman Empire, is despised by many of its subjects. You cannot force European cultures, languages and traditions into one. The Roman Empire was divided, and when the EU's strongest military force and its second largest economy, Great Britain left, it was weakened (Daniel 2:41-43).

"If you want to know a secret, it is this. The blessing from past revivals in Britain protected it from being submerged into an empire at odds with God. This blessing came from previous generations" (Exodus 20:6).

"Will the Antichrist appear from the European Union?" I asked.

"On the ruins of ruins and on the times of times," said the angel.

"I don't understand," I replied.

"Empires and unions have come and gone. Millions live on the ruins of empires and states which once felt invincible. Many believers have said, 'This is it.' But times and seasons change; empires crash and burn. This is the truth; the enemy is ever seeking to find 'the power' through which the Antichrist can arise."

"How close are we?" I asked.

"With the one world government will come an attempt to create a single monetary union, the foreshadowing of which is already upon you. You have seen the world beginning to form zones of influence and association. Things are moving fast and nothing is set in stone. Prayers and revivals change times and seasons, and the revelation of Antichrist can be restrained."

Chapter Eleven

Media, Martial Law and Antichrist

The revelations of the unfolding events flowed in a series of news reports and editorials. They hailed the man I understood to be Antichrist as a selfless hero, one who solved every problem under his leadership. Public opinion was highly favoured because the media primed them to adore him.

"Why are you showing me these events through the news, papers and social media?" I asked the angel.

"You experience your world through the media," he explained. "You listen to debates, political arguments and take sound bites to repeat to others. You read and think you are informed but you are not. How much of your speaking is independent thought and how much is parroting what you've heard in the media? Who is controlling whom?

"There's an elite who shape the thinking of billions. If they choose to focus on one subject they're interested in, millions suddenly care and repeat phrases like dictation machines. People become campaigners, resisters, bloggers, influencers and activists. They are not thinking for themselves. They are acting the role the elite want them to play. It's manipulation.

"Preconception, political bias, distortion, favouritism, worldview bias, preference, simplification, exaggeration and fabrication poisons the media. The biased media plans to make people think, believe or do things they otherwise would not. They are the grand puppet masters, orchestrating the symphony of people's thinking.

"Most of the protestors, activists and campaigners of today are the fodder of the elite. The billionaires, global political leaders, elite professors and CEO's of corporations decide the direction of the world. Then they command their workforce to brainwash the masses to believe and act in accordance with their will. They own half of the world's wealth and most people's opinions!

"Teaching rebellion against God's will, controlling others and manipulation is witchcraft. If you tell a lie once, people won't believe it. If you repeat it over and over from various sources of power, it becomes the new truth. The thoughts of the sheep of the world's pasture are owned by the wolves called the elite. They control them from the inside by thinking for them (1 Samuel 15:23).

"If these people were born in Nazi Germany or Stalin's Communist USSR, they would believe what they were told. The most troubling fact of history is how dictators easily found millions willing to murder and abuse in their name.

"The prince of the power of the air has anointed the lies of the elite with a demonic empowering, to get people ready to embrace the Antichrist when he comes. Over ten times in the Bible God affirms He does not want believers to be ignorant. Days of desperation will open the door to Antichrist and the media will train hearts to receive him (Romans 11:25, Ephesians 2:2, Revelation 12:9).

"The Antichrist will be seen as the greatest problem solver of his generation. He will be beloved, but as the world falls into deeper chaos, his aggressive nature will take hold. Before he can rise to power, Western ideals about freedom must be subdued to allow Antichrist to rise unchallenged. The media will love him, but those who challenge him will be silenced."

I silently watched echoes of events that I saw before, this time focused on the U.S. and of an unprecedented nature. National debt spiralled, banks collapsed as unrivalled chaos followed. With the exchange of goods and services paralysed, people could not purchase the necessities of life. Food stores were ransacked and they introduced Marshal Law. Natural disasters, meteorites and earthquakes continued to wreak havoc. The San Andreas Fault, running from San Diego to San Francisco was still torn apart.

Overnight the military took direct control of civilian functions. Troops occupied key towns and cities, and heavily-armed patrols surrounded government buildings, power stations, utility centres, food distribution warehouses, schools, airports and financial institutions.

Soldiers received power to stop and search all, and military checkpoints severed highways. Transport hubs were closed and roadblocks became common. Protests were banned, and every person was expected to provide proof of identity and a reason for travel. Curfews forbade people from leaving their designated areas and stay at home orders before dusk were issued.

Schools, shops and businesses closed for weeks as the military sought to regain order. Anyone seen out at night or crossing over their designated boundary was arrested. Peaceful armed civilians were compelled to surrender their weapons or be fired-upon. Corrupt military leaders had power to hold special tribunals to compel people to comply. Outside of the cities and towns, the government confiscated lands and established fenced camps to house people in tents from ruined parts of cities. They arrested anyone who seemed suspicious or threatening without trial. All the norms of the rule of law disappeared.

"Fear is the most inexpensive way of dominating people," revealed the angel, "the fear of arrest compels people to obedience."

A representative of the Union spoke on an emergency distress signal. "The last few years have tested our resolve like no other time in history. Natural disasters, the economic squeeze, shortages and pressures have challenged normal life. Then the earthquakes struck from the Great Californian Quake to the Ring of Fire. The loss of life and destruction of our infrastructure has changed our lives.

"Some proclaimed these worldwide disasters to be the end of the World Union. Those who pronounced such things did not take into account our resolve to stand fast, to overcome and prevail. Like never before, our American friends find themselves to be part of a global community, interdependent and integrated in ways all did not comprehend.

"When America was strong it came to the world's aid. Now the United States is weakened and it is time to repay the favour, as our Union comes to its aid. Banks will be re-capitalised, aid packages will be received, and emergency food, oil, and medical supplies are now on the way. The infrastructure will be rebuilt with Union equipment, which the United States lost to other countries in the economic rebalancing of the past.

"The United States, the most reluctant nation to join our Union, is discovering the hope of global integration. Their strength will be our fortitude. Our strength will be theirs. We are one world, one power and one in unity" (Revelation 13:1, 17:3, 9).

The man spearheading the extensive rebuilding of the United States with Union money and power was the Head of the Catastrophe Emergency Management Agency (CEMA). He brought global strength to work with the Federal Emergency Management Agency (FEMA).

Many months passed and life in the United States was returning to a new normal. Troops receded and civilian control re-emerged in a new form, as supplies were established. The news media and Hollywood celebrities praised the World Union for restoring the new normality to America.

"Powerful statements were made in the media declaring that without Union money, aid, supplies and help with infrastructure, order could not have been established at speed. Hollywood and influencers praised the Second Marshall Plan to rebuild the United States with World Union aid. In the political crisis which followed in the House and Senate, a Constitutional Convention was called. In days of strife, a two-thirds majority was found to add a new amendment to the Constitution, which allows for shared sovereignty with the World Union.

"I can't believe it," I said. "I thought most Americans would never accept joining a World Union."

"It was an economic crisis which paved the way for Hitler to take over Germany," said the angel. "As history teaches, when global events make people poor, millions will vote for anything if it gives them food and hope. But remember this; it took many years for Germans to be primed to accept Hitler. Before the Antichrist comes, the spirit of antichrist will use lost souls to prepare the way for him to be welcomed with open arms. Hollywood, the media and the entertainment industry will play a key role in brainwashing people to accept the Antichrist as a hero. Those who rebel against God will love the greatest rebel."

"They don't have that much power," I replied.

"They already use their power to sway the minds of the young to reject biblical values and embrace leaders who promote post-Christian values."

"Can it really be that bad?"

"Hollywood is a cult," he replied.

"They just make movies," I said.

"Hollywood celebrities and their shadowy leadership have been brainwashed into believing in the superiority of post-Christian values. The woke are morally broke. No evidence or the failure of their ideas will quash their blind faith.

"Victims of thought-control, Hollywood stars are bombarded from the beginning of their careers by powerful charismatic cult-type leaders who discourage thinking. When they declare their political opinions, they do so to an audience of clapping cult members. They think they are rebels, heroes to be celebrated, but they are cowards. In Hollywood, the individual is submerged into the collective mind. They say easy things to those who already agree with them and expect applause.

"In Hollywood, being tolerant means turning a blind eye. They accept everything because they value nothing. Their money provides them with an escape. They can fly away on private jets to their mansions. They have nothing to fight for and nothing to defend, except their lies, because they cherish nothing of the Christian values and freedoms that others won for them.

"All cults prey on the vulnerable and no one is more vulnerable than a child in the womb; they weep and call it a baby when they want the child, then they sneer at life and call it a foetus when it hinders them from making money. Unborn babies are God's children, not a choice. The ancients sacrificed children to Molech for their prosperity and today they are sacrificed for the same reason. It is human sacrifice renamed" (Leviticus 20:2-5, Psalm 139:13-16).

"Can we win these people to the Lord?" I asked.

"The Lord has a few in Hollywood whom He has reserved for Himself. They have not bowed the knee to Baal. The Lord has witnesses everywhere (Romans 11:4).

"The control of information and ideas will be central to the agenda of the Antichrist. The internet at first enabled people to communicate without censorship, but big tech companies can ban and censor those they disagree with, and governments can shut down social media platforms when they want. In the end times, the ability for people to share ideas on mass will be severely limited, as events from the Heavens silences them.

"In the end times expect signs in the sky," continued the angel. "Think of the echoes in history. In the summer of 1859, an astronomer in Kew, London, looked through his telescope and saw two patches of intensely bright white light exploding from the sun. That night, radiant lights were observed in the sky across North America and beyond, but then the telegraph communication systems began to fail. This was a Carrington Event, a solar flare with the energy of ten billion atomic bombs exploding, spewing subatomic particles and electrified gas towards earth. The Victorian world, still without electric lights and with limited electrical equipment survived with little damage.

"But the modern world could not cope with another geomagnetic storm from space! It would render useless power grids, electrical equipment, technology, satellite apparatus, GPS systems and radio communications. Those parts of the world worst affected by this space storm would be without electricity for prolonged periods. In 2012, a warning was conveyed to earth, when a similar coronal mass ejection passed the planet. If it hit, your interconnected world of communications would break down, allowing a few to control all information, power and influence. Putting everything online seems like a brilliant idea, until online ends; suddenly everything stops."

Chapter Twelve

The Temple Rebuilt

"There can be no end times without the Temple being rebuilt," explained the angel. "All things must come full circle; the past must meet the present and the end the beginning. Where Abraham sacrificed, the Lord must once again stand."

"I saw the Temple preparations when I was in Jerusalem," I stated.

"Solomon built the First Jewish Temple which stood for four centuries before Nebuchadnezzar II destroyed it after the Siege of Jerusalem," stated the angel (2 Kings 25:9).

"The Second Temple was modestly built by Zerubbabel on Mount Moriah, where the remains of the First Temple lay in ruins for seven decades (Ezra 3:8, 6:6-18).

"Then, before the Lord was incarnated, Herod planned for the Second Temple to be overhauled and refurbished, which took forty-six years according to John. This was accepted by religious leaders on the understanding that the offerings and sacrifices would never stop. This is why Herod's Temple is also known as the Second Temple. This last Temple, with humble beginnings, stood for close to six centuries" (Mark 13:1-2, John 2:20).

"Soon, the Third Temple of Jerusalem will be built!" declared the angel. In the Spirit, I was drawn to the Temple Mount in Jerusalem and looked down upon a rebuilt House of Prayer, with the Israeli prime minister giving a speech to a host of Jewish dignitaries.

"As a people and nation, we have always desired peace with our neighbours, even if this peace was at the cost of our own rights," said the prime minister. "It is well known that I have never supported rebuilding the Temple because peace with our Muslim neighbours is too important. In our love of peace, we were willing to sacrifice our historic land and our only site for true worship, for the good of posterity. We have cherished the hope of our children's peace with our neighbours, more than our right to pray on our ancestral land, where our forefathers worshipped.

"But four years ago an event took place which changed the heart of our nation. On that fateful day, when a meteorite fell from Heaven and destroyed the Dome of the Rock something changed within us all. Some Muslims saw this as a sign from God. Jews and Christians saw a gaping hole ready to fulfil biblical prophecy. Religious and secular Jews united, to recall the dream of our forefathers, that one day the Temple would be rebuilt!"

The prime minister spoke with tears.

"We all have ancestors who suffered throughout the centuries in Europe and beyond. In their deepest dreams, was the hope of a homeland.

He paused.

"At the heart of our homeland is the Temple of Promise. One day, we aspired to be free to worship our God in our ancestral home, in peaceful security and friendship with our neighbours.

"When the meteorite hit, it was a sign from Heaven. A new spirit was birthed in us, as we wept the tears of our ancestors. Our enemies told us building a Temple would be a provocation. But I will remind the world, that all religions have their special sites – but not us, the Jews. Only we have been denied the sacred home of our faith. We Jews have been forbidden to possess the Mount of Promise, where our forefathers worshipped for centuries. How can any deny the hope of our people?

"Today I stretch out a hand of peace to our Muslim neighbours. I remind them the Dome of the Rock was a shrine and not a place of worship. The Al-Aqsa Mosque on the Temple Mount is being restored at the cost of Israeli taxpayers (Ezekiel 40:17, Revelation 11:2).

"All the world has their own place of worship! Now we the Jews, have our own. Jeremiah the Prophet foretold these days and I am struck by these words of his: 'I will make an everlasting covenant with them, that I will not turn away from doing them good; but I will put My fear in their hearts, so that they will not depart from Me. Yes, I will rejoice over them to do them good, and I will assuredly plant them in this land, with all My heart and with all My soul' (Jeremiah 32:40-41).

"We, the people of God have been planted in this land by Him and we are the benefactors of His everlasting covenant, which God made with our forefathers. In this Temple, we will recommit this nation to God and honour His promise to us."

"The Temple will be rebuilt!" I exclaimed.

"The New Testament is clear the Temple must be rebuilt," said the angel. "How can the Man of Sin sit 'as God in the Temple of God, showing himself that he is God,' if there is no Temple in Jerusalem?" (2 Thessalonians 2:4).

"He can't without a Temple," I said.

"How can the end time Abomination of Desolation prophecy be fulfilled without a Temple?" (Daniel 12:11-12, Mark 13:14-15).

I shrugged my shoulders, saying, "It can't."

"Listen to the vision of John and remember the Scriptures must be fulfilled: 'Then I was given a reed like a measuring rod. And the angel stood, saying, "Rise and measure the Temple of God, the altar, and those who worship there. But leave out the court which is outside the Temple and do not measure it, for it has been given to the Gentiles. And they will tread the holy city underfoot for forty-two months" ' " (Revelation 11:1-2).

"But what about the sacrifices in the Temple, they cannot be restarted," I said. "Christ is the final sacrifice! He gave the ultimate sacrifice for sin. The price is paid" (Hebrews 10:1-38).

"You are sure of many things," said the angel, "but how little true knowledge you have. The sacrifices of the Temple continued for at least three decades after Christ's final sacrifice. Since the fall of the Temple in AD 70, devout Jews have been waiting for sacrifices to resume (Deuteronomy 12:4-6, 8-11, 13-14, Psalms 51:20-21, Malachi 3:4).

"Many generations of Jews have forgotten the need for blood sacrifice. When the offerings commence again, it will prepare their hearts for the revelation that the only sacrifice needed has already been made by Christ (1 Corinthians 5:7).

"Have you already forgotten the revelation given to Hosea? The Scriptures declare: 'For the children of Israel shall abide many days without king or prince, without sacrifice or sacred pillar, without ephod or teraphim. Afterward the children of Israel shall return and seek the Lord their God and David their king. They shall fear the Lord and His goodness in the latter days' (Hosea 3:4-5).

"This prophecy speaks of the latter days, this means the end times. When Hosea gave this prophecy the sons of Israel had everything. It was inconceivable for them to lose their king, Temple and the items within, and yet all this came to pass.

"The prophecy states for they 'shall abide many days' without a king and sacrifices. This has come to pass and remains for two thousand years. Yet, as the revelation states in the last days, they will return to God seeking Him and by doing so, they will also seek David their King – who is Jesus Christ" (Matthew 1:1).

Time passed in a vision and there was rioting around the Temple, and the media bitterly criticised the presence of the House of God in Jerusalem and its daily animal sacrifices (Daniel 8:11).

The prime minister of Israel gave an urgent address about the violence and international condemnation:

"Our ancient Scriptures preserved in the Dead Sea Scrolls, prophesied this Temple would be rebuilt," he said. "Long have been the preparations and the Third Temple now stands as a symbol of peace.

"I call upon all leaders in the world to support Israel's right to worship on the same ground of our forefathers – just as you do in Westminster Abbey in London, or in St Paul's in Rome. We too have a right to worship freely; to live in peace and to possess our land. Muslims have Mecca and we cede the Al-Aqsa Mosque in peace.

"We have respected your rights, now we ask for you to respect ours. I urge all nations, let the Jews worship in our holy place in peace. Show us the tolerance we have shown you."

The status of the Temple of Jerusalem became the

prime issue that the media focused on. News reports showed rioting throughout Israel, the Middle East and worldwide. They beheaded people in Muslim areas and outrage grew at the sacrifices in the Temple. The media manipulated public opinion to grow hostility towards Israel and millions marched in protests globally (Ephesians 2:2, Revelation 20:4).

The minister responsible for law and order throughout the World Union gave a press conference. He spoke of his regret at the loss of life and added, "In these exceptional days of crisis it is essential for law and order to be maintained. We cannot allow the Middle East to fall into deeper chaos.

"Israel has aggressively rejected our invitation to join the fellowship of this World Union and must cease its confrontational behaviour. The Temple in Jerusalem is an illegal anathema to the peace of the nations.

"We will seek with all efficacy to find a peaceful settlement. But if Israel refuses to heed international law and align itself with peace, it may be necessary to use Union forces to restore order. The shedding of blood on the streets of the Middle East must cease with immediate effect. We must seek the greater good to end the violence. I repeat, if we find no peaceful resolve to the provocation, the Union has the power to enforce international law in Israel and on the Temple Mount" (Revelation 6:9-11).

In the Middle Eastern nations and countries with mixed multitudes of faith, where Jews and Christians are the minority, they were attacked and died in numbers during multiple riots.

"The persecution of the Church and the suffering of Israel are interconnected in the end times," said the angel. "As pressure builds on Israel, it will build on Christians too. The Church is grafted into the Vine; as it happens to one, so it happens to another" (Romans 11:23-27).

Chapter Thirteen

Rise of the Antichrist

There was a large auditorium and a man on the stage was receiving praise for saving the United States from collapse, after several natural disasters shook it to pieces. Awards were given and a Nobel Peace Prize was accepted. Celebrities endorsed him and social media was filled with his praise. Documentaries and films hastily occupied people's screens and indoctrinated them. They claimed his leadership skills saved tens of millions around the world, as he directed Union resources to rebuild the global economy and its infrastructure.

"The Antichrist will be a highly skilled politician," said the angel. "He will be an inspirational speaker, able to charm people out of their freedom. By flattery he will deceive and corrupt (Daniel 11:32).

"After he has risen to full power, his speeches will fail to convince all and the Antichrist will use force to compel obedience. He will begin in peace by respecting faith. But his actions will grow aggressive until he magnifies himself above all that is called god. As he reaches his zenith, the full revelation of evil in him will be unveiled, as he speaks blasphemies against the God of gods" (Daniel 11:33-39).

"Should we expect the Antichrist in our lifetime?" I asked.

"Your prayers and witness empower the Restrainer; they are holding back the power of Antichrist. The longer the antichrist spirit is bound souls can be saved. The Restrainer will be taken out of the way when it is God's perfect time (2 Thessalonians 2:6-7).

"Antichrist is the false messiah. He is the rotten gift for those who reject the true Messiah. Those who spurn the Christ will get what they asked for: the false Christ. He is their punishment. In the meantime, the Restrainer is powerful enough to suppress the spiritual powers of darkness seeking to promote the Man of Sin."

"What more should I know about the Restrainer?"

"The witness of the Holy Spirit in the Church is restraining evil," said the angel. "When believers are taken to meet the Lord in the air in the Rapture, this restraint will be removed. But the Holy Spirit is everywhere. He will continue to work on earth during the Tribulation period; convicting souls, anointing them and filling them. He is the Spirit of revival" (Revelation 7:13-17).

"I hope the angels will help," I said.

"The angels serve in a ministry which is not fully revealed to humanity. But to Daniel it was revealed the Archangel Michael protects Israel. In the end times, he will be withdrawn for a season to let evil do its bidding."

"That's a sad thought."

"If Michael remained, the enemy would be restrained forever," said the angel. "The Antichrist must have his time, as the world learns the true cost of sin. Then Michael will arise to fight for God's will and the Antichrist will be overthrown with Jesus' return" (Daniel 10:13-21, 12:1, Zechariah 1:10-11, Jude 1:9, Revelation 12:7).

"Please tell me the key turning point," I begged.

"The moment to watch out for is the revelation of the Abomination of Desolation and what follows will be irreversible" (Daniel 11:31, 12:11, Matthew 24:15-22, Mark 13:14, Revelation 12:7-10, 12-14).

There was a gathering of the leaders of the nations. It was the G7 of this age, and presidents and prime ministers of the ten great zones of power met to plan the future. Their discussion focused on the man I knew to be Antichrist, the Head of the Catastrophic Emergency Management Agency (CEMA).

The Chancellor of Germany, representing tens of millions of Europeans spoke, "For hundreds of years individual nations have fought for the self-interest of their people, to the detriment of others. By imposing sanction on troubled nations, we alienated the weak. When we fought or indeed lost wars, we punished the losers economically and militarily. By thinking of ourselves first, we sowed seeds for future conflict," she said.

"After the two World Wars, Europeans came together

working for common goals in peace. The European Union was not strong, with its feet of clay, but we are the benefactors of its divided inheritance; we have learnt from its mistakes and rebuilt. Nor have we forgotten the cost of the great conflict with China; afterwards we vowed never again to pay such a price for division. Competing interests are at odds with respect for humanity.

"Now, in our time, unprecedented troubles have hit our nations. We struggled apart to respond. Nations and regions on their own could not solve our international problems. It was the global nature of this struggle that drew us together.

"We called for each part of the world to come together into regions of friendship, just as Europeans did. When these ten zones of power formed, we began to solve complications with greater speed. We discovered global problems need global leadership. This is why the ten regions joined in deeper ties. Our economies were already interlinked; now our political will is joined to form a greater Union of friendship."

The people clapped and cheered.

"When natural disasters destabilised the world, we worked together to overcome. We have met these challenges and shall overcome those which remain. We have been bruised, battered and shaken, but our faith in our common humanity has grown. The arc of history bends toward unity.

"But our troubles are far from over. We have been tested like never before, and in the last few years we discovered again, that our competing national interests have led to division, battles and fighting. Our Union is strained. But to those who choose bigotry over unity, I say, your time is over!"

The room echoed with celebration.

"Those who reject the momentum of history have forgotten the basic tenants of this Union. If one of us falls, we all fall. If one is hurting, we all hurt. We are all in this together; one world, one economy and one humanity.

"We have learnt to our detriment how red tape, political division and promoting national interests hurt all. When one region withheld vital aid in global disputes, we all suffered. Something has to be done and this is the reason we have met together today. We need a fresh approach; we tried to find this path before, but we were not ready.

"After years of negotiations, we have reached an unstoppable conclusion. The leaders of this great Union have resolved to choose one person to possess emergency powers to address our immediate global challenges. From our ten regions, one individual will be chosen to embody the values and beliefs of our great Union. In this person, we will invest power to move with haste, with no red tape, to solve our abundant global emergencies. The full force of the Union will be at his or her disposal, as a servant of peace."

There was silence and confusion in the room.

"For years we have debated, discussed and presented our candidates in private. But this crisis is deep. We cannot spend more time debating, issuing statements and blocking aid with red tape. We must act.

"History is heavy upon our shoulders. Destiny calls. Future generations demand we must rise to this challenge. Some have said, 'This is the end of democracy.' To them I say, 'No, no and no!' "

"Julius Caesar, dictator in perpetuity," shouted an American.

"This is no time for obscure constitutional debates and making one country great again," snapped the chancellor. "These emergency powers will be given, under restraint, for the good of all. Those who oppose this move don't understand the urgency of the hour. If we don't act now, we won't have cities, countries, homes or jobs to fight for. We are fighting for our survival."

The silence on the floor was broken by a few people clapping, which slowly broke into applause.

"We have asked, 'Who should be entrusted with such power to act without red tape?' The answer was already in our hearts: The one who has been found faithful. The only person suitable to hold said power is the one who doesn't want it – the humble servant forerunner. We the leaders of the ten regions have only one name upon our lips!"

The angel whispered, "These are of one mind and they will give their power and authority to the Beast" (Revelation 17:13).

The speech continued, "He is one of us and all of us. He is a Syrian-American by birth, European by culture, Chinese by philosophy and Indian in religious tolerance. He has served in Africa, South America, Australia and the United States.

"He toiled in secret as the head of the Union's Catastrophic Emergency Management Agency (CEMA). It was he who directed our universal resources to bring order and stability back to many towns, cities and nations. Millions already owe their lives to him. But many do not know his name.

"The leader of CEMA has chosen to be a man in the shadows because he does not want fame. He does not desire an elected office and it's precisely because he shuns the limelight, that he is the only one suitable to exercise this power.

"He is us and we are him. His interests are our interests. He has toiled sacrificially when no one was watching and now his deeds are honoured in the light.

"This man is uniquely qualified. It was his fast-acting decisions that restored electricity, water, gas and food supplies in the United States. He helped Americans, Africans and Australians; he can now help the world! We have not chosen an amateur but an expert. As one of the holy books says, 'He who is faithful in what is least is faithful also in much' (Luke 16:10).

"Only those who do not want power are trustworthy to possess it. This is such a man. With the signing of this new treaty, the entire might of our global Union will be at his disposal. No more forms to fill in or debates as people die in the streets, waiting for help from the aftermath of earthquakes, fires, solar flares and the meteorites which have weakened us" (Revelation 13:4).

The ten leaders representing the ten regions of the world signed the treaty and the Antichrist was sworn in as President of the Union. I expected him to look evil. He didn't. Charm and grace flowed from him. Many resisted but a demonic swarm caused people to love him upon a glance. Evil was being called good.

The Antichrist gave his inaugural address and I overheard a few phrases. He said, "I am a humanist, a Christian and a Jew; I am Muslim and Buddhist. I am a follower of all religions and all philosophies. I am a servant of tolerance. Together, nothing will be impossible for us" (Genesis 11:6).

This man was not one of the ten global leaders but was beloved of them. He was the eleventh. When he spoke, he mesmerised people with his words. In a shocking turn of events within the first week, he scolded three of the ten leaders for their incompetence. He insisted they should be sacked. They were unpopular for their failings in their nations and he won over people with his skill. With the power granted to him, he replaced them immediately and did it with applause (Daniel 7:24).

The angel said, "There was another horn, a little one, coming up among them, before whom three of the first horns were plucked out by the roots. And there, in this horn, were eyes like the eyes of a man, and a mouth speaking pompous words" (Daniel 7:8).

The Antichrist convinced all that the most powerful office in the world should be centred in Rome. He reminded them Africans, as well as Europeans, once led the Roman Empire. He recalled how Africans, Asians and Europeans fought together as one in the Roman Age. He said, "The city of Rome sits on seven great mountains and these mountains represent the seven continents of the world. From the seven mountains, we will make decisions to save the seven continents" (Revelation 17:9).

Most of the population of earth believed this exchange of power had little to no real influence upon their lives. It was just paperwork. Despite the unfolding crises, the days turned over and those who could work, study or shop continued, and when supplies arrived in Union trucks to those without, all were grateful.

It surprised me how life for millions worldwide felt the same. Presidents and prime ministers led their nations, as long as they submitted to the directorship of Antichrist. The military and police received riot training or were sent overseas. Finding evidence and delivering justice came second to establishing order. The Union took a great interest in the economy, and factories with important goods were told to deliver products at the command of the Union.

In many parts of the world there were uprisings, rejecting the handing of power to Antichrist. Some states in the United States rebelled against taking orders from this popular world leader. Many spoke openly about secession from the United States and the World Union.

There was a great rebellion in London, England, with Parliament Square occupied by protesters holding signs declaring, 'Magna Carta, our liberty,' and, 'Habeas corpus, fair trials.' Troops moved in to disperse the crowds with tanks, but before it was complete, a shocking earthquake struck the city. The clock face of Big Ben collapsed down to street level and the great bell fell into the River Thames. It felt symbolic. The Mother of Parliaments folded in on itself.

Much of the Muslim world was now embracing radical Islam and called for a Jihad. I couldn't believe the media was still proclaiming the Antichrist a Man of Peace, as wars were being fought to resist his rule. Wherever there was resistance, Union forces and locals fought until towns and cities were left in ruins. The media seemed unconcerned about the troubles. It was like the forgotten conflicts of our age, where the media chooses to omit what's happening because it doesn't fit their narrative.

In those areas which refused to submit to the Antichrist regime, a pattern unfolded. They cut all means of communication as people protested; phones, radio, TV, social media and the internet went dead.

The only message which could be received was from the Antichrist system. Emergency broadcasts sent a message that terrorist elements were rising against the government and people were ordered to stay home for their safety.

The streets in many regions were flooded with military vehicles. Civilians outside were forced home. Soldiers were sent to the residences of powerful people to detain political leaders, preachers, authors and broadcasters.

The speed of this transfer of power was overwhelming. Within twenty-four hours, the world turned upside down. They placed all areas which resisted into military lockdowns. Fear seized people's hearts. Helicopters flew overhead, jets scrambled and the sounds of explosions in the distance were heard.

Elite soldiers indoctrinated by the Antichrist media were ordered to seize unsympathetic leaders in the military and replace them. These young soldiers like Hitler's youth believed they were paving the way for peace. With the Antichrist system in control of the military worldwide, a purge followed. Those who questioned what was taking place were detained and disappeared. Those queuing for food and water from Union tankers were too busy trying to survive to notice.

Chapter Fourteen

Self-Censorship

A few months passed and a new equilibrium was formed. Just as Europeans found a way to survive Nazi occupation, those living under the new world order found their rhythm of life.

Once people accepted the role of Antichrist – who seemed to be a charismatic, secular world leader – a new understanding was formed. Many believed this system was successful. Needs were being met, order was restored and life was settling down. Rebellions continued, but like Syria, some cities were flattened, whilst others carried on like nothing was happening.

The new world order reminded me of the first few decades of the Soviet Union. Whilst the West was diminished by the Great Depression beginning in 1929, the propaganda of the Soviet Union was claiming abundant harvests and production.

"From what I understand of history, great unions of nations tend to fail," I said to the angel. "The Soviet Union produced poverty for the masses in the name of equality and a wealthy corrupt elite."

"The end time one world government has been likened to the Roman Empire," he replied. "History has separated you from that empire. You have forgotten the Roman Empire was a forced, uneven and often unstable alliance of peoples. It was forged by the harsh realities of the day.

"Daniel was shown the foundations of an empire, including legs and feet of iron, mixed with clay. It was precarious and likely to break apart at the right time. He also saw a fourth Beast; this is the shadow of the end time empire of ten powerful regions of the world, working as one with the Beast, in the spirit of the Roman Empire (Daniel 2:33-34).

"The Bible says, 'After this, I saw in the night visions and behold, a fourth Beast, dreadful and terrible, exceedingly strong. It had huge iron teeth; it was devouring, breaking in pieces and trampling the residue with its feet. It was different from all the Beasts that were before it and it had ten horns...the ten horns are ten kings who shall arise from this kingdom' (Daniel 7:7-8, 24).

"As with ancient Rome, so with the end times," declared the angel.

"It's bizarre to think people will fall for this deception," I said.

"The signs are in the shadows," he asserted. "All dictatorships thrive on people denying their conscience. It begins with 'self-censorship.' It happens when the government and the media create an atmosphere where people feel afraid to speak the truth. Everyone knows the lie, but no one is willing to address it.

"You have many examples of censorship in your time. Those who speak the truth are forced off platforms that love lies. Many journalists spin their stories to fit an agenda; they are anti-Israel and anti-Christian because they are antichrist. As they love darkness instead of light, they are not educating people but indoctrinating them. They are playing into the hands of the antichrist spirit."

"I pray believers will not be silenced," I said.

"The politically correct hostility created by the elite has created self-censorship in your age," replied the angel. "People feel compelled to censor their sense of right and wrong. They are afraid of being cancelled and shamed for speaking facts. The antichrist spirit cannot win an argument against truth. This is why censorship is part of the end time strategy. Those with a voice can expose Antichrist's lies. Those who are censored cannot.

"Breaking down the individual's ability to speak and be heard is a major step towards preparing the way for the Antichrist system. We find the genesis in the attack on free speech, leading to self-censorship. This is because Satan needs the conscious to be silenced to advance his agenda. When Christians are silent, the witness and restraint will diminish, and the generation which welcomes the Antichrist can arise!

"But in the future, all free media will be closed or nationalised by the state. The Antichrist will not accept free expression or criticism. Soldiers will storm conservative media outlets where they can and in other places, their bank accounts will be frozen, ending their ability to persevere."

"I think most Christians will never accept Antichrist," I said. "They cannot be fooled this easily."

"They were fooled before," insisted the angel. "Germany was once at the heart of Bible-believing Christianity. However, when Hitler arose quoting the Bible and speaking about God, many Christians believed him. By 1933, the German economy was on its knees and over thirty percent of the population was unemployed. Hitler promised the German people salvation from their troubles. People ran to him, despite all the warning signs. They heeded their eyes, not the discernment of spirits (1 Corinthians 12:10).

"To get the support of Christians, Hitler evoked God in many speeches. He said in 1937, "In this hour, I would ask of the Lord God only this, that He would give His blessing to our work, and that He may ever give us the courage to do the right.' He told Christians what they wanted to hear and made them feel he was one of them.

"For many Christians, Hitler seemed to be the man God sent to save Germany from the misery of the shadow of the Great Depression and the shame of the Treaty of Versailles. Christians voted for and supported Hitler, but the spirit upon him was evil. He locked his true intentions inside.

"Under the Nazi system, the German economy boomed and government income rose by fifty percent in ten years. Almost all the six million unemployed in 1933 found work and by 1939, only 302,000 were unemployed. Hitler created an economic miracle! Then he began to wrestle back lands that were lost to Germany, without at the beginning, a shot being fired.

"Whilst Hitler was planning to murder millions of Jews, Christians gave thanks for him in their churches. They loved him because he gave them jobs and pride in their nation.

"Churches continued to preach, sing and pray as normal, just as an antichrist figure was laying the foundations for their ruin. Jesus warned the elect can be deceived and millions were in Germany. Those who resisted were imprisoned or killed (Matthew 24:24).

"Hitler was under the influence of the antichrist spirit, but he was not the Antichrist," explained the angel. "Think of the teaching of John: 'Little children, it is the last hour; and as you have heard that the Antichrist is coming, even now many antichrists have come, by which we know that it is the last hour' (1 John 2:18).

"Adolf Hitler was a type and forerunner of the Antichrist. He came as a secular leader delivering a few years of incredible economic growth and military success, followed by total disaster. A similar thing will happen to the Antichrist.

"First, there will be successes, then three and a half years of achievements in troubling times will follow in the first half of the Tribulation, superseded by three and a half years of total meltdown. The same pattern of prosperity and disaster was seen in Nazi Germany" (Revelation 11:2, 13:5).

Chapter Fifteen

Salvation from the Tribulation

There was a large church and an African American pastor was speaking to his congregation. He was well known, but his time has not yet come. I thought, he is yet to be born.

"This book is God's Word," he said, holding a Bible in the air. "I believe Jesus Christ is the Way, the Truth and the Life, and salvation is found in no other name, but Jesus" (John 14:6, Acts 4:12).

The congregation shouted, "Amen," and throughout his sermon people clapped, cheered and shouted in agreement.

"But we are living in days of great deception. Many of us have grown up believing we were born into a 'Christian nation.' But the Bible warns a day is coming when good will be called evil and evil good (Isaiah 5:20).

"The Scriptures warn of an evil time: A time when people who stand for truth will be called liars! A time when families who stand for Christian values will be rejected and hated.

"This time is now. Many of you sitting here have been forced to appear before tribunals at work for what they call discrimination. They call you intolerant and bigoted.

"God foretold a day was coming when our government would become so hostile to Christian values, that it would become impossible for us to remain inside the system (Revelation 13:16-17).

"Step by step, we have moved towards this day. The level of intolerance aimed directly at Christians by the advocates of tolerance is alarming. Jesus said, 'If the world hates you, you know that it hated Me before it hated you' (Luke 21:17, John 15:18).

"We preachers saw this coming decades ago when the mockery of the Christian faith became acceptable. Those who follow foreign gods were granted special protection by the media. But filmmakers, TV producers, recording artists and comedians were permitted to bitterly attack the core beliefs of Christianity, teardown our Christian heritage and blaspheme the noble name of Jesus Christ.

"Our politicians have quoted the Bible to get votes, but they ignore God's Word in their legislation. Step by step we have been slowly returning to the days of open persecution. But remember this, when they hate you, it is not truly you they hate, but God in you. They hate that you have sided with God against sin (Matthew 10:22, 24:9, Mark 13:13, Luke 6:22, 21:17).

"We have been on a slippery slope for decades and it has led to the Antichrist rising to power. The day of open persecution has begun. We have suffered intolerance and persecution is rising. Yet, I believe God will save us from the coming Tribulation!

"If we are obedient and resist what the devil will soon try to do through Antichrist, God will come for us. The Bible says, 'For God did not appoint us to wrath, but to obtain salvation through our Lord Jesus Christ, who died for us, that whether we wake or sleep, we should live together with Him' (1 Thessalonians 5:9-10).

"God saved Noah from the flood and Lot was saved from Sodom. We shall be saved too. God established this truth with Noah and He reconfirmed it with Lot. There is a principle in the Bible that the righteous will escape God's wrath.

"For we have not been appointed to wrath, but to obtain salvation by faith in Christ's death and resurrection! Listen to the words of Jesus, 'Watch therefore and pray always that you may be counted worthy to escape all these things that will come to pass, and to stand before the Son of Man' (Luke 21:36).

"Think on the revelation to Nahum. In the first chapter filled with the outpouring of the wrath of God, we are told this: 'The Lord is good, a stronghold in the day of trouble and He knows those who trust in Him' (Nahum 1:7). God is the stronghold during the time of wrath and He will save all who trust in Him.

"The Antichrist may be in power now, but God will judge him and we are going to take refuge from God's wrath because of His endless mercy in Christ (Psalm 4:3).

"We are not with the lost, but the saved! Christ is our hope in the day of doom! We are not waiting for God's judgment, but His redemption. We are expecting to see God's Son from Heaven, whom He raised from the dead, even Jesus who delivers us from the wrath to come (Jeremiah 17:17, 1 Thessalonians 1:10).

"Do not be afraid. We will be delivered from God's wrath because we have already been delivered in Christ. The Scriptures are clarion: God will set a seal on those who love and obey Him. Ezekiel heard the Lord say to His angel: 'Go through the midst of the city, through the midst of Jerusalem, and put a mark on the foreheads of the men who sigh and cry over all the abominations that are done within it' (Ezekiel 9:4).

"You have wept over your nation. You have sighed as the nations voted for a man who is the Antichrist. The Lord hears your sighing. Yes, the end time period is a time of trouble, but it is also a time of Holy Spirit outpouring! Many will be saved. God is throwing out our baby milk bottle and giving us strong meat (1 Corinthians 3:2, 2 Peter 2:7-8).

"The Church is being sifted by fire. Those who once attended churches, but did not believe have fallen away. They didn't want their names to be on the list the government is making. They are like Lot's sons-in-laws. Lot tried to warn them, but they were unspiritual. They laughed when they should have fled (Genesis 19:14).

"Those who have fallen away are trying to rebuild a lifestyle which will never return. The destruction is too great. These people who called themselves 'Christian' are like the foolish virgins. They knew the Lord was coming, but they have no oil in their lamps. When Christ comes they will rush to be ready, but it will be too late (Matthew 25:1-13, Luke 17:26-36).

"We have suffered from man, but God will not let us suffer His anger. The Lord Jesus said, 'Because you have kept My command to persevere, I also will keep you from the hour of trial which shall come upon the whole world, to test those who dwell on the earth' (Revelation 3:10).

"Those who have fallen away have committed spiritual adultery. They will go through the Tribulation to give them time to repent. But those who have repented will escape this time of God's judgment. Remember, it is he who overcomes who will be saved (Revelation 2:22, 3:5).

"In the Tribulation to come, there will be 144,000 new converts who will bring in a harvest for Jesus. The Lord will provide for these dear souls because without the Mark of the Beast, they cannot buy or sell. Can you see why the Lord encourages us to pray for our daily bread? It is to prepare believers to look to God alone for provision during the time Antichrist takes over the economy (Revelation 13:17).

"These are dark days, but the full might of the Antichrist system has not yet reached us; we still have some freedoms. We can pray, despite his growing power. In our country the police are being purged of the honourable and outspoken believers are being arrested. But the Lord is on our side, He is fighting for us.

"I urge you now, put your heart right before God. Purge the sin now. Come fully under His Divine protection. Repent of all known sin and turn to Jesus Christ. He is our strength in time of trouble. He is our Provider. The King of kings is fighting our battle!"

After the sermon, I was shown the news. The media produced a segment on his message. They showed edited footage of his preaching, providing selected sound bites. They twisted the pastor's words to make him appear angry and they mocked him as an extremist, and he was arrested for inciting violence.

"It's not right," I said.

"As you now understand, the elite who control the media will welcome the Antichrist," said the angel. "Freedom will end with cheering. When disaster was close to Sodom and Gomorrah, those who were warned laughed" (Genesis 19:14, Revelation 16:9, 11).

"At least preachers will stand firm," I said.

"For every preacher who stands against Antichrist, there will be pastors, vicars, bishops and Christian ministries who will quote Scripture urging Christians to support him" (1 Peter 2:13-14, Revelation 2:10, 20:4-6).

Chapter Sixteen

Peace Treaty with Israel

The Antichrist began his career slowly gathering power and drawing greater authority to himself. Outwardly he appears to be a charming problem solver who must settle the greatest quandary: The status of Jerusalem, with the controversial Third Temple.

At first, his exercise of jurisdiction over the nations will seem distant. Each nation has its own leader, but all were taking instructions from him on the direction they needed to take. This was expressed as synergy. The theme was one of global cooperation, not dictatorship. Meanwhile, resources and military might were being drawn to him. Normal citizens of the nations continued their lives unaware of the true scale of the events unfolding.

I watched the Antichrist growing in power, as He gave speeches on peace, disarmament and the bond of all religions. His tone on faith changed as he grew in power. When all was at his feet, he mocked faith in God as a source of division and promised faith in humanity is the solution.

The media presented the Antichrist as a man with the seasoned charm and the sophistication of a 1950s Hollywood star. He argued effectively that changing times and laws were necessary, for the ten regions of the world to synchronise harmoniously. He changed the legal framework of the nations to allow the Antichrist to harness the economic and military might of the world (Daniel 7:25).

This power was at first given to him to respond to natural disasters. But once power is given, it's hard to return. Purges of senior leaders continued to take place. Some were major politicians and global leaders; others were influential people from the civil service. The media portrayed the purge of those hostile to Antichrist as removing the incompetent and harnessed public opinion with its influence. In some cases, one accusation from a person, with no evidence, was enough for the media to smear the individual and force him or her to resign.

Most of the people believed the lie they were sold. This Man of Peace was not stealing power in their eyes, but harnessing it for them, for the good of mankind. He was solving world problems with the resources which belonged to all. As long as their lives got better, did it matter?

Increasingly the speeches of the Son of Perdition urged that nationalism, faith and belief in local laws or constitutions were holding people back. He argued the World Wars resulted from people loving their nation and its laws above others. Freedom was an illusion if millions are slaughtered in global conflicts. He declared true liberty was deliverance from war. To achieve peace, all which divides must be disregarded and going to war with those who resist would lead to peace.

As time progressed they passed new laws to ban what was called 'Christian extremism.' Anyone who resisted the Antichrist system, based on the Bible was regarded as extreme. The 'radical Christians' were hindering world unity and their leaders needed re-education. Preachers who refused to go on courses concerning open-mindedness and candidly confess the constitutions of the past were troublesome, disappeared into secret prisons. This was no time for Habeas corpus; normal freedoms are suspended in times of crisis.

Antichrist thus became the man of lawlessness. Whatever laws hindered his plans fell at his whim. But he remained popular, as the Scriptures foretold: 'Through his cunning he shall cause deceit to prosper under his rule and he shall exalt himself in his heart' (Daniel 8:25, 2 Thessalonians 2:8).

The Antichrist was a shrewd political manipulator. He used flattery and deceit to get his way. He gave speeches on what he called 'The Greatest Geopolitical Problem on Earth,' which he identified as the State of Israel. He blamed the Jewish State for injustices, wars and instability in the Middle East.

It surprised me how few resisted his ideas. The media had primed the public to perceive Israel as intolerant, unjust and illegal. Through economic boycotts and sanctions the prime minister of Israel was forced to the negotiating table with Antichrist, the head of the nations (Daniel 11:32).

Suddenly the angel spoke, "The antichrist will sign a seven year peace treaty with the government of Israel and he shall divide the land for political gain" (Daniel 9:27, 11:39).

"The Antichrist will achieve peace in Israel!" I exclaimed.

"His greatest achievement in the eyes of the world is the nail in his coffin in the eyes of God," pronounced the angel. "Zechariah foresaw this end time peace treaty, saying, 'And it shall happen in that day that I will make Jerusalem a very heavy stone for all peoples; all who would heave it away will surely be cut in pieces, though all nations of the earth are gathered against it' (Zechariah 12:3).

"By dividing the land of Israel and Jerusalem, the Antichrist and all with him will join an end time stronghold of demonic power. If you read your Bible, you will understand that events in the natural correspond with outcomes in the spiritual realm (Job 1:6-7, Daniel 7:26, Zechariah 3:6-14, Revelation 16:5-7).

"God owns everything, He is the Creator and He is the One who gave the land of Israel to His chosen people forever. Why do the nations rage against Him? The reason, as you are learning, is that Jesus will return to Israel. He is coming to restore God's chosen people and nation. Thus, if Satan can divide and annihilate Israel, he thinks he can destroy God's end time plan. Satan knows the survival of the Jewish State is crucial to God's plan for the last days (Isaiah 40:1-66:24, Zechariah 14:3-4, 8-9, Acts 1:6-7, Romans 10-11, Galatians 6:16, Revelation 7:4).

"Therefore, when politicians and religious people support the division of Jerusalem, they are seeking to divide the inheritance of Jesus Christ. No other people, tribe or nationality has any claim on Jerusalem other than the Jews (Nehemiah 2:20).

"Christian denominations which make declarations concerning Israel's need to divide the land are openly rejecting the will of the God they claim to serve. They are aligning themselves with the spirit of antichrist, who will force Israel to give up land for a false claim to peace. They are rejecting God's Word. The branch which was grafted-in must not boast against the root (Romans 11:17-36).

"Churches who try to break God's covenant with Israel will be broken. God will put them to shame. Their leaders will spend their days closing down buildings and selling off land, instead of expanding" (Psalm 129:5, Revelation 1:20, 2:5).

"In the Old Testament over forty times God uses Scripture to confirm He has given the land of Canaan to the people of Israel (Genesis 24:7, 26:2-5, 50:24-26, Exodus 6:8, 13:5,11, 32:13-14, 33:1, Numbers 11:12, 14:16,23, 32:11, Deuteronomy 1:8,35, 6:10,18,23, 7:13, 8:1, 9:5, 10:11, 11:9,21, 19:8, 26:23, 26:15, 28:11, 30:20, 31:7, 20-23, 34:4, Joshua 1:6, 5:6, 21:43, Judges 2:1, 1 Chronicles 16:15–18, Nehemiah 9:15, Psalm 105:8-11, Jeremiah 11:5, 32:22, Ezekiel 20:6, 28, 42, 47:14).

"Three times God confirms the gifting of the land to Israel is forever and His covenant with Abraham is unbreakable. Therefore it is 'an everlasting covenant.' Thus, when God gives the title deeds of a land to a people of His choosing, woe betide anyone who rejects God's will. Whenever Israel is forced by a foreign power to give up land, that very land becomes a staging post to attack Israel (Exodus 32:13, Psalm 105:9-12, Judges 2:1, 1 Chronicles 16:15-18).

"Many nations, peoples and empires have tried to occupy and divide the land of Israel in history. Each one has in time been divided, weakened and broken up. For years the prophecy of Zechariah has found a partial fulfilment, as the nations of the world rage against God's plan for Israel. In the end times, the prophecy will be completely fulfilled (Zechariah 12:2-3).

"Why do the nations rage and the people plot a vain thing? The kings of the earth set themselves, and the rulers take counsel together, against the Lord and His

Anointed, saying, 'Let us break their bonds in pieces and cast away their cords from us.' He who sits in the Heavens shall laugh. The Lord shall hold them in derision. Then He shall speak to them in His wrath and distress them in His deep displeasure: 'Yet I have set My King on My holy hill of Zion. I will declare the decree: The Lord has said to Me, "You are My Son, today I have begotten You. Ask of Me, and I will give You the nations for Your inheritance and the ends of the earth for Your possession. You shall break them with a rod of iron, You shall dash them to pieces like a potter's vessel" ' " (Psalm 2:1-9).

"All spiritual eyes must watch Israel," I accepted. "But I fear the horror of the Tribulation."

"There are four significant reasons why the Great Tribulation will fall upon earth," asserted the angel.

"The first is for dividing God's land. You cannot take Israel and Jerusalem against God's express will, without falling into deep judgment.

"The second is for judgment upon those who persecute Christians: 'Since it is a righteous thing with God to repay with Tribulation those who trouble you' (2 Thessalonians 1:6).

"The third is for failing to acknowledge God as the source of all life (Job 33:4).

"The fourth is for refusing to obey the gospel of Jesus Christ. The Lord will come 'in flaming fire taking vengeance on those who do not know God and on those who do not obey the gospel of our Lord Jesus Christ' (2 Thessalonians 1:6, 8).

"As for Christian denominations, I give you this great warning: Either you are working with God and supporting His plan for Israel, or you are fighting against Him. Those who will resist God will not go unpunished. The Prophet Isaiah proclaimed Israel was to be forsaken for a season and gathered again, and it was. Now everlasting kindness is their heritage (Isaiah 54:7-8).

"The Church must heed this warning: Do not confuse Israel with the Church. God's covenant of peace is not unmovable. Just as you cannot move a mountain, so you will not move God's promises with Israel. In the end, those who fight against Israel will be defeated. The Lord promises: 'For I will contend with him who contends with you' (Isaiah 49:25, 54:10-15).

"God has told the Church to pray for the peace of Jerusalem and lasting peace will only come when Jesus Christ returns as the Messiah-King. Therefore, all prayers for the peace of Jerusalem are prayers for the return of Christ" (Psalm 122:6).

"Maranatha," I exclaimed.

"The Book of Revelation describes a great war breaking out in Heaven and Satan was cast out," said the angel. "The first thing Satan did after falling was to persecute God's chosen people and nation. In Israel, God will finalise the past, the present and the future (Revelation 12:7-9, 13-17).

"What the Church needs to ask itself is this: Are you standing with the Saviour who intends to redeem Israel? Or are you standing with the spirit of the Antichrist, who intends to divide Jerusalem and overcome Israel? Christians will be judged in this matter and eternity will weigh your actions."

Chapter Seventeen

The Rapture

Three people were sitting outside. Without warning, time froze. At this moment the clouds above their heads tore open, revealing bright shining stars, planets and moons. One of these individuals turned to look at another, but she was lifted into the eternal realm at speed, soon unaware of anyone (Mark 1:10, Revelation 6:14).

In the Heavenlies, her eyes opened to a new reality of love, peace and joy. After a timeless season to acclimatise, she was brought into a large space. God the Father was sitting on His mighty throne, with thousands of angels around and Jesus Christ at His right hand. The Lord was clothed with a garment down to the feet and girded about the chest with a golden band. His head and hair were white like wool, as white as snow, and His eyes like a flame of fire. His feet were like fine brass, as if refined in a furnace and His voice as the sound of many waters (Ezekiel 1:24, Revelation 1:13-15, 14:2).

The woman was called to stand before Jesus by the angel. The Lord gazed at her with a warm smile and confessed her name to God the Father. The words of Jesus came to mind, 'Therefore whoever confesses Me before men, him I will also confess before My Father who is in Heaven' (Matthew 10:32, Revelation 2:17, 3:5).

Judgment proceeded with the Lord, calling forth all her acts of faithfulness to Him. Her secret giving, prayers, exploits of kindness and endurance were mentioned. When judgment was complete, she was given a new name and a place was reserved for her at the Marriage Supper of the Lamb.

"Do you understand what you saw?" asked the angel.

"I wish I did," I said.

"There are three great judgments coming," explained the angel. "One for believers, another for Tribulation survivors and the end of the age judgment."

"Will Christians be judged in all three?" I asked.

"The first is the Judgment of Believers at the Judgment Seat of Christ," the angel replied. "This is what you saw. This judgment is not for access to salvation, but for what Christians did with their salvation (2 Corinthians 5:10, 1 Peter 1:17).

"The second is the Sheep and Goat Judgment for those who survive the Tribulation and those raised from the dead afterwards. This will take place at the beginning of the Millennial Reign and the greatest issue will be how the nations treated Israel (Matthew 25:32).

"The third is the Great White Throne Judgment, when all the dead will be brought back to life to face the last judgment. This will happen just before earth's ultimate destruction. The fallen angels will also be judged just before this time and thrown into the everlasting fire (John 5:28-30, Jude 1:6, Revelation 20:7-15).

"There is much to look forward to for believers, but the Lord gives a warning to those who are not righteous. The angels 'will gather out of His Kingdom all things that offend and those who practice lawlessness' " (Matthew 13:41).

"At what point will believers be Raptured?" I asked.

"All who died in history as true believers in Jesus will be raised by Christ when He returns first for His Church. This is called the Resurrection of the Just by Jesus and the Day of Redemption by Paul. He also calls it the Day of Christ (Luke 14:14, Ephesians 4:30, Philippians 2:16).

"When Christians are Raptured they will be transformed in the twinkling of an eye. These believers will meet the Lord in the air. Due to the speed of the Rapture, non-believers will not see Christ or His people leave. They will suddenly disappear; one second they will be there, the next they're gone. Listen to the words of Jesus, 'Then two men will be in the field: one will be taken and the other left. Two women will be grinding at the mill: one will be taken and the other left' (Matthew 24:40-4, John 14:1-3, 1 Thessalonians 4:13-18).

"This is what the Bible says about this time: 'When Christ, who is your life appears, then you also will appear with Him in glory.' At the Rapture, all true believers in

Jesus will be immediately given new imperishable, glorified bodies (Colossians 3:4).

"The Lord will come for His Church with the dead in Christ by His side, the Church will be Raptured and the graveyards will be emptied. All the bodies of those who died in faith will instantly be raised and glorified. Thus, all believers will have total redemption – spirit, soul and body will be redeemed, and combined as God planned" (1 Corinthians 15:51-57, 1 John 3:2).

"Amen!" I replied.

"The Lord is returning to save His children from the coming Tribulation," said the angel. "There is a reason believers will be Raptured before the seven year Tribulation. This is because Jesus has already drained God's wrath for them. The Bible says, 'Having now been justified by His blood, we shall be saved from wrath through Him' (Romans 5:9).

"If the Lord came for His Church during or after the Tribulation, people could try to predict His expected return, based upon the Abomination of Desolation. People could use the seven year Tribulation period to plot Jesus' return for His Church. This will not happen. No one knows the day or the hour. This also means no one can predict the year or decade" (Mark 13:32).

"Many have tried," I replied.

"It is God's will for you to know the signs of the times," said the angel. "But the Lord warns that no one knows the day or the hour of His return for His Church for an important reason. You may believe you understand the times, but the Lord will return at a season you do not expect. Do not think you have a special code or understanding to track the timing of the Lord's return. No one knows; expect the unexpected" (Matthew 24:44).

"As I have explained, if believers press in for revival, they can postpone the revelation of Antichrist because new Christians will resist his coming. Thus, the things you see are what could happen, depending on the prayers of believers. Remember how Abraham pleaded and Zoar was saved for a season? He was told, 'See, I have favoured you concerning this thing also, in that I will not overthrow this city for which you have spoken.' Nineveh was also given a reprieve because of Jonah's preaching. But destruction came to both at a later time" (Genesis 18:16-33, 19:21-25, Exodus 32:14, Jonah 3:1-10, Nahum 1:1-14).

"What will happen to believers who are Raptured?" I asked.

"You have already had a glimpse. The Judgment of Believers, called the Judgment Seat of Christ in Scripture, follows the Rapture of the Church and the resurrection of the bodies of those who died in Christ (Romans 14:10-12, 2 Corinthians 5:10, 2 Timothy 4:1).

"At this moment, true Christians will be upgraded to become Sons of the Resurrection. As faith in Christ justifies believers, this judgment concerns what they did with their salvation; did they serve Him honestly and faithfully? What did they do with their gifts and talents? This is explained clearly by Paul. For the Lord 'will bring to light what is hidden in darkness and will expose the motives of the heart. At that time each will receive their praise from God' (Luke 20:36, 1 Corinthians 4:5).

"As I have told you, the Judgment of Believers concerns rewards for faithfulness, not access to salvation; true believers in Jesus Christ will stand blameless before God (1 Corinthians 1:8, Ephesians 2:8-9, 2 Timothy 4:8).

"Christians will be judged by God before the judgment of non-believers and their actions weighed because judgment 'begins with us first.' The Lord's Divine fire will test all the works of Christians. Everything which proceeds from wrong motives will fail. Peter explained believers will be judged 'according to each one's work' (1 Corinthians 3:10-15, 1 Peter 1:7-9, 4:17-18).

"Paul identified Christians with wrong motives: 'If anyone's work which he has built endures, he will receive a reward. If anyone's work is burned, he will suffer loss; but he himself will be saved, yet so as through fire' (Matthew 16:27, Luke 16:10, 1 Corinthians 3:14-15, Revelation 1:14-15, 22:12-17).

"The purging of all your works at the Judgment Seat of Christ is also referred to as the Day in the Bible. To prepare for this hour, Jesus said believers must give to those who cannot repay, concluding: 'And you will be blessed, because they cannot repay you; for you shall be repaid at the Resurrection of the Just' (Luke 14:14, 1 Corinthians 3:13).

"The Judgment of Believers does not focus on 'how much work' you did for the Lord, but the motives of one's heart. Did you obey God out of sincerity or did you serve for the praise of people? 'Therefore judge nothing before the time, until the Lord comes, who will both bring to light the hidden things of darkness and reveal the counsels of the hearts. Then each one's praise will come from God' (1 Samuel 16:7, 1 Corinthians 4:5, Hebrews 4:12-13).

"In Matthew 25, Jesus notes two separate judgments. The first is the Judgment of Believers (Matthew 24:27-25:30).

"The second is the Sheep and the Goat Judgment at the beginning of the Millennial Reign. Both times the Lord references His coming. The first is like lightning followed by Tribulation; the second is for all to see and the Millennial Reign will begin (Matthew 24:27-29, 25:31-45).

"Jesus said, 'Behold, I am coming quickly and My reward is with Me, to give to every one according to his work...he who overcomes shall be clothed in white garments, and I will not blot out his name from the *Book of Life*; but I will confess his name before My Father and before His angels' " (Matthew 24:36-25:30, Revelation 3:5, 22:12).

"Many will fear falling short," I confessed.

"The Lord does not despise a broken and contrite heart. However, the sin that is cherished is exceedingly dangerous, whilst the sin which one seeks to overcome is covered. The grace of God is being renewed towards you daily. All who walk in the light will be cleansed daily from their sin" (John 1:7, 16).

"What about those who desire to love God with all their heart and end up failing miserably?"

"There are some who will be saved as through fire" (1 Corinthians 3:15, 5:5).

"Help me understand this," I implored.

"In the passage of Matthew 24:27-31, Jesus reveals the Rapture first, then the Tribulation. Afterward, He will come for all to see Him and judge the world. This is the beginning of the Millennial Reign. Then in Matthew 25, during the genesis of the thousand years of peace, Jesus speaks of His judgment of the nations."

"This is deep," I confessed.

"Jesus comes first for His Church and the Tribulation will begin on earth," explains the angel. "Believers will be in Heaven at this point and it is there the Judgment of Believers will commence" (Revelation 19:8).

"The Rapture of the Church is first," I said.

"Christians will receive rewards in Heaven, whilst the Tribulation is taking place on earth (1 Corinthians 4:5, 2 Timothy 4:8, 1 Thessalonians 4:17).

"After the Lord Jesus Christ has rewarded Christians for their faithfulness, the Church will celebrate the Marriage Supper of the Lamb in Heaven. With believers judged, rewarded and joined to Christ, they will be ready to join Him to rule under His authority during the Millennial Reign (Song of Solomon 2:4, Matthew 22:1-14, Luke 14:15-24).

"Just before Christ's return to earth for all to see, John is shown believers celebrating with rewards from God. The Rapture has taken place, the Marriage Supper of the Lamb is underway and the saints are preparing to return with Christ to earth.

"Listen to John's description: 'And I heard, as it were, the voice of a great multitude, as the sound of many waters and as the sound of mighty thunderings, saying, "Alleluia. For the Lord God Omnipotent reigns! Let us be glad and rejoice and give Him glory, for the Marriage of the Lamb has come, and His wife has made herself ready." And to her it was granted to be arrayed in fine linen, clean and bright, for the fine linen is the righteous acts of the saints. Then he said to me, "Write: 'Blessed are those who are called to the Marriage Supper of the Lamb!' " ' (Revelation 19:6-10).

"During this period Jesus will call believers by name. The Lord said, "The one who is victorious will, like them, be dressed in white. I will never blot out the name of that person from the *Book of Life*, but will acknowledge that name before My Father and His angels" (Revelation 3:5).

"It can be confusing," I acknowledged.

"Let me say it plainly," said the angel.

"Three times God will judge people. The three separate times are defined by the seat which Christ sits on during judgment.

1. "The Judgment of Believers will take place before 'The Judgment Seat of Christ' in Heaven during the Tribulation on earth (Romans 14:10, 2 Corinthians 5:10).

2. "The Sheep and Goat Judgment of the nations at the beginning of the Millennial Reign will take place by Christ 'on the Throne of His Glory' (Matthew 19:28, 25:31).

3. "The judgment of everyone else will take place when God brings all humans who ever lived back to life before the Great White Throne Judgment" (Revelation 20:11).

"Deep truths," I said.

"The end time period is hard for humans to understand," said the angel. "But God has revealed His plans on purpose because He wants you to know. However, when all is said and done, the end times can be simplified in one important statement of fact for those not Raptured:

"All will die, all will be raised from the dead and all will be judged by Jesus Christ."

"That's clear enough," I replied.

"The only issue which counts is this: Are you ready? As a believer, you must get ready for the Rapture by purifying your heart. Jesus spoke of those left behind and said, 'Watch therefore, for you do not know what hour your Lord is coming. But know this, that if the master of the house had known what hour the thief would come, he would have watched and not allowed his house to be broken into. Therefore, you also be ready, for the Son of Man is coming at an hour you do not expect' " (Matthew 24:40-44).

"It's going to be mighty strange when tens of millions of Christians disappear," I said.

"You have read the parable of the wise and foolish virgins many times. The first interpretation identifies the importance of the individual being ready to meet Christ. Are they filled with the Spirit, trimmed and ready to meet the Bridegroom? There is a deeper meaning" (Matthew 25:1-13).

"I am willing to learn," I said.

"In the Bible, oil represents the anointing of the Holy Spirit. A church without the Holy Spirit is dead. The lampstand represents a church in the Book of Revelation. When Christ comes those churches without the Holy Spirit will have their lampstands removed" (1 Samuel 16:13, John 14:26, 15:26, 16:7, Ephesians 4:30, Revelation 1:20, 2:5).

"How does this apply to the end times?" I inquired.

"The true Church will be taken by Christ during the Rapture. The dead church will remain and the Apostate church leaders will be used by Satan to find a simple explanation why millions of Christians disappeared. By lying, they will hinder the salvation of many. Their lie will cover their unregenerate hearts.

I watched as a bishop gave an announcement on the disappearance of millions of people worldwide, "I believe these Christians who disappeared were inflicted with a terrible infection," said the bishop. "Christians tend to go to conventions together and visiting preachers do the rounds of churches. This is why the infection has been limited to some Christian circles. This is a tragedy and nothing more. Science will help us understand why their bodies disintegrated with speed. Science will provide the answer. For those who speak of a great Rapture, I say you are on unsound theological ground.

"Our calculations suggest seventy percent of Christians are still active in churches. Most services continue as normal, with a few absentees in each. We mourn each life that was lost. This was a terrible virus which caused hallucinations for those who watched the fast disintegration of bodies. There was no Rapture!

"Whilst we mourn those we lost, we also give thanks to our mother god for protecting those who remain. Our churches will remain open for prayer for all faiths and we will pray for the President of our Union to guide us in tough times."

"The Rapture is a blessing for the disciples of Jesus," said the angel, "but it will lead to a curse unfolding on the earth. When the Church is Raptured, there will be no one left to restrain the Antichrist. The loss of the witness of the Holy Spirit in the Church will allow the Man of Sin to exploit and destroy. With one mind, those left behind will accelerate the plans of the evil one.

"Some will realise they made a deal with the devil and many will be saved out of the Tribulation. But at the end of the Tribulation period, Jesus will give the command from Heaven for the restoration of the Jewish people to Himself. The Valley of Achor will be a door of hope" (Isaiah 25:6-8, Hosea 2:15, 2 Corinthians 3:15, Ephesians 4:18).

Chapter Eighteen

The Tribulation

The international media celebrated in Jerusalem, witnessing the signing ceremony between their beloved leader, known to me as Antichrist and the prime minister of Israel. The Son of Perdition was called the Man of Peace and the hero who solved the greatest conflict in modern history. It was clear from the body language of the prime minister of Israel that he was not pleased with the deal, but was forced by the sheer weight of the economic and political burden the global community put on him.

"With the signing of the peace treaty which divides Israel and Jerusalem, the nations of the world will have openly rejected God's will," warned the angel. "It is not their city to divide! Listen to these words and let them sink into your soul, 'The Lord has chosen Jerusalem' (Zechariah 3:2).

"The nations have now deliberately divided the land which God warned they must never do. Therefore, with the measure they forced God's people to divide the land in Israel, so their lands will be divided by earthquakes and disasters (Genesis 13:15, 1 Chronicles 16:15-19, Ezekiel 38:4, Hosea 8:7, Joel 3:2, Zechariah 12:2-3, Matthew 7:2).

"This act of splitting Jerusalem is the announcement of the genesis of the seven year Tribulation. The beginning of the troubles is at an end, the Tribulation is launching. Look out for the seven great signs of four which shall shake the nations!"

"Seven signs of four," I repeated.

"This dark season coming upon the whole world will 'test the inhabitants of the earth.' The peoples of the world no longer fear the Lord and God will send His Tribulation to evaluate mankind. Those who hear His voice will repent and sin no more. Those who refuse to fear the Lord will be judged" (Exodus 20:20, Revelation 3:10).

"I'm in awe," I said.

"The end time prophecies in the Bible document the annihilation of all antichrist systems of governance on earth. These antichrist systems are already in place in your time, waiting to give their power to the Antichrist."

"Christians must resist," I said.

"The judgment coming during the Tribulation will lead to a greater disintegration of the world economy, the devastation of the infrastructure and significant loss of life. Your green and pleasant land will become charred with darkened skies!

"This end time Babel system must fall, resulting in the loss of all trust in mankind's ability to rule and reign without Christ. The coming disasters will finally prove to all who survive their absolute dependence on God Almighty!"

"I pray many will be saved," I said.

"The Tribulation is the countdown to a new beginning, the end of an old order, to prepare for the new. Just as Sodom and Gomorrah were reborn in your time, so will fire from Heaven fall and destroy these systems. Listen to Isaiah: 'They declare their sin as Sodom; they do not hide it. Woe to their soul! For they have brought evil upon themselves' (Isaiah 1:10, 3:9).

"The Sodom and Gomorrah generations have no shame in sin. They rejoice in their wickedness and declare what God has called an abomination, as good. To be holy is oppression to the generation of Sodom (1 Corinthians 6:9, 2 Peter 2:6).

"The destruction of Sodom and her sister was a forewarning. The disintegration of normality during the Tribulation will be the fullness of wrath. There will be a stricter judgment for those who lived where the gospel was proclaimed. Jesus said, 'Assuredly, I say to you, it will be more tolerable for Sodom and Gomorrah in the Day of Judgment than for that city.' The wealthiest and most luxurious will be judged harshly for wasting their wealth on the passing pleasures of sin" (Mark 6:11, Revelation 18:6-7).

"I hope mankind turns to Jesus," I said.

"The Scriptures confirm most of mankind will not turn from their sin, therefore the Tribulation will be measured out in kind for wickedness (Daniel 12:10).

"Heed the prophets: Obadiah declared, 'For the Day of the Lord upon all the nations is near; as you have done, it shall be done to you; your reprisal shall return upon your own head' (Obadiah 1:15).

"Ezekiel foresaw the affliction: 'Son of man, when a land sins against Me by persistent unfaithfulness, I will stretch out My hand against it; I will cut off its supply of bread, send famine on it and cut off man and beast from it' (Ezekiel 14:13).

"But Zephaniah proclaimed those who repent during times of judgment will receive grace: 'It may be that you will be hidden, in the Day of the Lord's anger' " (Zephaniah 2:3).

"The imagery of the Great Tribulation in the Bible is hard to understand," I confessed.

"All the imagery you see in the Bible concerning the Tribulation represents spiritual realities in the Heavenlies, influencing events on earth. You will not see the Four Horses of the Apocalypse in the Heavenly realms, but you will see the result of their actions. Look out for the sign of sevens."

"Open my eyes," I asked.

"Seven is the perfect number. There will be a piercing series of judgments coming in sevens and they will grow in intensity! There are four sets of sevens to end all things.

"Seven seals to be broken.

"Followed by seven trumpets.

"Before the sounding of the seventh trumpet, there's the mystery of the seven secret thunders.

"Then, the seven bowls of wrath."

"Seven seals," I said, repeating what I heard, "seven trumpets, seven secret thunders and seven bowls of wrath."

"These are the four signs of seven to draw people to repent before the end," said the angel. "However, four times the Bible records the majority of the people will refuse (Revelation 9:20-21, 16:9, 11).

- 106 -

"The prevailing culture of this age is revealed in Scripture. They will not repent for making idols of man, worshipping false gods and demons. People will not repent for their abortions, murders, sorceries, thefts and sexual immorality. They refuse to give God glory or repent of their blasphemies and evil deeds. They will continue to mock God's Word and witness. They follow the path of sin because they love the evil antichrist system which rejects all God stands for (Revelation 14:10, 11:18).

"Jesus warned the blood of all the prophets from Abel to Zechariah would be required of a single generation and you can read in history what a great price they paid! The blood of all who have been killed in innocence will be required of the last day generation. Justice must be done (Isaiah 26:21, Luke 11:50-51).

"The spirit of judgment and burning will cleanse the land. But those who receive Christ during the Tribulation will find a covering. There is always a refuge in the Lord (Isaiah 4:4-6, 26:20).

"Nevertheless, they have hardened their hearts to stone and they will refuse to even consider the disaster unfolding as a sign of Christ's return. They will blame the crisis on the failure of politicians to address global warming and environmentalism.

"They will declare the Tribulation is not a sign from God because they do not believe in Him; then in the next breath they will curse God. They will be spiritually blind to all these events. Jesus foretold their spiritual blindness, saying, 'and they knew nothing about what would happen until...' " (Matthew 24:39, Revelation 16:9).

"Can you help me understand the four sets of judgments?" I asked. "What are the seven seals, the seven trumpets, the seven secret thunders and the seven bowls of wrath in the Book of Revelation?"

"Beware the Four Horsemen of the Apocalypse," said the angel. "Zechariah was the first to see the Four Horses moving with speed and shaking the nations. In such a manner, the seven seals of Revelation all have a specific meaning (Zechariah 6:1-8).

"The first seal: The White Horse represents Christ the

King of kings and Lord of lords going out conquering to conquer. The Lord rides on a pure horse, the first of the Four Horsemen of the Apocalypse. There is purity in the gospel. Salvation and redemption are offered to all who will repent during the Tribulation period. This is why Christ will stay ahead of the three terrible horses of conflict, shortages, famine and death. The offer of salvation must come first (Revelation 6:1-2).

"The second seal: The Red Horse represents great conflict on earth. Mankind will learn how terrible it is to hate others. Peace will flee with wars, genocide and terror (Revelation 6:3-4).

"The third seal: The Black Horse represents death through famine. This will be a time of great scarcity. When John received this revelation, a denarius was the daily wage for a working man. He predicts prices will rise tenfold for essential goods. However, the rich will still have their luxuries, such as the 'oil and wine,' representing wealth (Revelation 6:5-6).

"The fourth seal: The Pale Horse represents widespread death on earth. Plagues and pandemics will lead to the demise of twenty-five percent of the population. Science will find no cure. Death will take the bodies, Hades the soul (Revelation 6:7-8).

"The fifth seal: The Antichrist will be permitted to overcome new converts in Christ for a season, those who repented after the Rapture. Many will be martyred for their faith and will cry to God who will bring them justice (Revelation 6:9-11).

"The sixth seal: There will be cosmic shocks. The largest earthquake in history will strike; islands will move out of place and mountains will collapse. Disarray will descend upon those who survive. The sun will grow dark, with an ash cloud in the sky and the moon will appear blood red (Revelation 6:12).

"The seventh seal: 144,000 Jewish followers of Jesus Christ will be chosen. They will be sent to preach the gospel in preparation for the opening of the seventh seal. Expect an unprecedented harvest. The first evangelists were Jews and the last will be Jews. When the seventh seal is opened there will be exhilarating silence in

Heaven for half an hour" (Revelation 7:1-17, 8:1).

"Troubling times," I said.

"The Lord explained if these days were not cut short, no flesh would survive. The judgments will be shortened to protect those who will repent during this time" (Matthew 24:22).

"Thank you Jesus," I exclaimed.

"After the seven seals are broken, seven angels will be chosen to sound seven trumpets. An eighth angel will hold a golden censer, offering it with the prayers of the saints.

"In the Temple of Jerusalem, the censer was used to burn incense and was replete with burning coals. The angel will take fire from God's altar, fill the censer and throw it to earth. This will happen in response to the prayers of God's people for justice from Antichrist. Then the trumpets begin (Revelation 8:1-5).

"The first trumpet will strike the vegetation on earth. Hail and fire will destroy a third of all trees and the grass will be burned (Revelation 8:7).

"The second trumpet will strike the seas. A great burning mountain of fire will be thrown into the sea. This will lead to an environmental catastrophe for all sea life. The world's greatest tsunami will sweep the nations and a third of all ships will be destroyed. Expect islands to split in two and one side will slide into the sea creating tsunamis, and underwater mountains will collapse. Jesus explained the seas and the waves will roar (Luke 21:25, Revelation 8:8-9).

"The third trumpet will make drinking water unclean. An asteroid called Wormwood will strike earth creating earthquakes and rogue waves. The debris in the air will lead to an impact winter. Sunlight will be blocked, little will grow and a third of all drinking water will be polluted by Wormwood. A third of all who drink this tainted water will die (Revelation 8:10-11).

"The fourth trumpet will strike the stars. A third of the sun will be struck, a third of the moon and a third of the stars will be darkened. The fallen angels will plummet (Revelation 8:12).

"Before the sounding of the fifth trumpet, an angel will

cry out for the woes coming upon earth. If people still refuse to repent during this period, the following three trumpets will be far worse" (Revelation 8:13).

"It will get worse!" I exclaimed.

"The fifth trumpet leads to Satan turning on his own and tormenting all who follow him in their rebellion against God. People will discover whom they chose to be their lord! Satan will be permitted to punish the citizens of the world by scourging them for five months. Demonic locusts from the bottomless pit will be released, and the sun and the air will be darkened. Mankind will seek death and fail to find it. All who repent and trust in Christ during this period will be spared further agony. These new believers will be sealed by God and protected from satanic torment (John 8:44, 10:10, 1 John 3:8, Revelation 9:1-12).

"The sixth trumpet will release four angels who are bound at the Euphrates. One third of humanity will die because they refuse to repent of their wickedness; they will be consumed by fire, smoke and brimstone" (Revelation 9:13-19).

"I hope many will repent," I said.

"Remarkably, those who survive these disasters will still refuse to turn away from their idolatry. They will not repent of witchcraft, drugs, addictions, sexual perversions, murders and thefts. The breakdown of society will prove the veil of civilisation is thin. Expect looting and lawlessness on an unprecedented scale (Matthew 24:12, Revelation 9:20-21).

"Before the seventh trumpet sounds, the apostle John was told of the secret of the seven thunders. He was not permitted to share these mysteries from the angel with a little book. At this point, there shall be no further delay and the mystery of God will soon be finished (Revelation 10:1-5, 6-7).

"John was also instructed to measure the Temple of God in Jerusalem, but he was warned to leave the outside court for the Gentiles. Two supernatural witnesses will be sent to earth to proclaim and they will be killed, but we will consider them later. Then the last trumpet will sound (Revelation 11:1-3).

"The seventh trumpet will be the Declaration of the Kingdom. The angel will proclaim all the kingdoms of this world have become Christ's and He shall reign forever. By the time of the sounding of the seventh trumpet, at least one third of the population of the planet will have died. Meanwhile, in Heaven, the twenty-four elders will praise God and the Temple of God will open, revealing the supernatural Ark of the Covenant" (Revelation 11:15-19).

"I hope this will be the end," I said, in exhaustion.

"No," replied the angel, "the wrath of God will be complete in the last seven plagues of the seven bowls. But before the end of all things takes place, those who have gained victory over the Antichrist will celebrate in Heaven" (Revelation 15:1-3).

"What will happen in God's Temple in Heaven?" I asked.

"Seven angels will come out of God's Temple in eternity with the last seven plagues," explained the angel, "and the Temple will remain closed until the wrath of God is complete. Many of the judgments which came upon ancient Egypt will be repeated, but this time on a larger scale" (Revelation 15:6-8).

"Which ones?"

"The first bowl is loathsome sores," replied the angel. "God's mercy is great and all who repent in this time will be spared the misery of the sores which will inflict many (Exodus 9:9-10, Revelation 16:2).

"The second bowl will defile the sea. The sea turns to blood and everything dies in its water (Exodus 7:17-18, Revelation 16:3).

"The third bowl will defile drinking water. All rivers and springs will turn to blood because Antichrist sheds the blood of the saints (Exodus 7:19-21, Revelation 16:4-7).

"The fourth bowl is an unstable sun. The sun will superheat resulting in mankind being scorched with fire. Your scientists have considered the possibility of such damage from a gamma-ray burst of an exploding supernova, from the WR104 star."

"This sounds like an extinction-level event," I exclaimed.

"The fifth bowl will bring darkness. The Antichrist Kingdom will be in darkness and mankind will seethe in pain (Exodus 10:21-23, Revelation 16:10-11).

"The sixth bowl will dry the River Euphrates. The dragon, the False Prophet and the Beast will draw their army to war against Israel at Armageddon. This army will cross the dry riverbeds of the region (Revelation 16:12-16).

"The seventh bowl will be the greatest earthquake in history. Jerusalem will be divided into three parts and the cities of the world will collapse. Hail will fall from Heaven" (Revelation 16:17-21).

"How can anyone survive this?" I wondered.

"If you are afraid," said the angel, "remember what the Lord said: 'Pray always that you may be counted worthy to escape all these things that will come to pass and to stand before the Son of Man' and, 'because you have kept My command to persevere, I also will keep you from the hour of trial which shall come upon the whole world, to test those who dwell on the earth. Behold, I am coming quickly' " (Luke 21:36, Revelation 3:10-11).

Chapter Nineteen

144,000 Sealed

"The four sets of seven judgments will begin when Jerusalem is divided by the nations," said the angel. "The breaking of the seven seals, the sounding of the seven trumpets, the mystery of the seven secret thunders and the outpouring of the seven bowls of wrath will continue, as the following end time events are unveiled.

"First, 144,000 will be sealed.

"Second, the Antichrist will break his treaty with Israel.

"Third, the Abomination of Desolation will defile the Third Temple in Jerusalem.

"Fourth, the counterfeit resurrection will deceive many and the unveiling of the Beast from the Sea.

"Fifth, two Supernatural Witnesses will prophesy, be killed, rise again after three days and ascend into Heaven.

"Sixth, Armageddon will begin.

"Seventh, Christ will return with His saints and Antichrist with his armies will be defeated."

"All of this will take place during the Tribulation judgments," I acknowledged.

"During the Tribulation, God will find 144,000 witnesses from the twelve tribes of Israel to complete the commission which the Church has taken lightly," explained the angel. "Jesus said, 'This gospel of the Kingdom will be preached in all the world, as a witness to all the nations and then the end will come' (Matthew 24:14).

"Why has the end not come? Because the Church has not finished the work! Therefore, God Almighty will call 144,000 evangelists from the twelve tribes of Israel, to reap a great harvest at the end of this age. Angels in the Heavenly realms will go to war and bind demonic powers keeping people bound in unbelief. Thus, the end time angelic witness of the gospel will bring in a great harvest

(Revelation 7:4-8, 12:7-8, Revelation 14:6-7).

"These evangelists will bring in the complete number of the Gentiles which must be saved. Only then will God restore Israel" (Zechariah 12:10, Romans 11:25).

I was puzzled and posed a question: "How can the 144,000 be found by God, when the lost tribes of Israel are still missing?"

"There are many who call themselves by many nationalities and yet God knows they are descendants of the lost tribes of Israel. I speak much of the children from the Middle East and the Mediterranean regions" (2 Kings 17:5-6, Joel 3:6-41).

"The lost tribes of Israel are not lost to God!" I uttered.

"God will speak to these descendants of the lost tribes during the Tribulation period and He will reveal Messiah to them. Many Muslims will find Jesus Christ, the Son of God. Do not underestimate how many people in the Middle East think of themselves as Muslim, yet they are God's. Many are children of the lost tribes! They shall be grafted back into the Vine; first as descendants of Abraham, then as believers in Jesus the Messiah. They will be called to be evangelists.

"Jesus said, 'And other sheep I have which are not of this fold; them also I must bring, and they will hear My voice; and there will be one flock and one shepherd.' Many are from the tribes of Reuben, Issachar, Zebulun, Naphtali, Gad, Asher, Levi and Manasseh, but there is a deeper mystery of the lost tribes of Revelation, which I will explain later" (1 Kings 5:26, 2 Kings 15:29, 16:9, 17:5-6, John 10:16).

"The Lord knows where the lost tribes of Israel are!" I said.

"The Church age began with the Jews proclaiming Jesus as Messiah and it will end with Jewish preachers, followed by the restoration of Israel. These 144,000 evangelists will be the most effective witnesses in history. They will bring in the last great harvest and Jesus will see the labour of His soul and be satisfied" (Isaiah 53:7-12, Revelation 7:9-12).

"I think some people will claim to be part of the 144,000, when they are not," I said.

- 114 -

"The 144,000 will have a specific holy lifestyle and anointing," explained the angel. "They will all be single and celibate, with a history of purity and speaking the truth. These men will not be afraid of death because they have nothing to lose. In the Tribulation, married men will focus on protecting their wives and children, but these preachers will not fear anything, including the Antichrist. Great signs and miracles will follow their testimony and they will win multitudes to the Lord (Revelation 14:4-5).

"Paul foresaw the great blessing which will cause the restoration of Israel, saying, 'Through their fall salvation has come to the Gentiles. Now if their fall is riches for the world and their failure riches for the Gentiles, how much more their fullness' (Romans 11:11-12).

"In the Book of Revelation, John witnesses a large harvest, which the 144,000 will win for Christ during the Tribulation period: 'After these things I looked and behold, a great multitude which no one could number, of all nations, tribes, peoples, and tongues, standing before the throne and before the Lamb, clothed with white robes, with palm branches in their hands...Then one of the elders answered, saying to me, 'Who are these arrayed in white robes and where did they come from?' And I said to him, 'Sir, you know.' So he said to me, 'These are the ones who come out of the Great Tribulation, and washed their robes and made them white in the blood of the Lamb' " (Revelation 7:9, 13-14).

"What is the deeper mystery of the lost tribes of Revelation?" I asked.

"When you read the Bible, did you notice the names of the tribes of Israel in Revelation chapter seven?"

"No," I replied.

"The tribes of Dan and Ephraim are missing from the list of the 144,000."

"I've never seen that before," I said.

"The tribes of Dan and Ephraim were the first to embrace idol worship in Israel," said the angel. "Dan sponsored a false priesthood which served idols and corrupted a Levite, and Ephraim followed. Dan also refused to fight for God's promises in the time of Deborah. For these reasons Joseph and his posterity replaces them. In the end times, the Lord will only choose those who worship Him in purity (Judges 5:17, Judges chapters 17-18, 1 Kings 12:28-30, 2 Kings 10:29).

"The 144,000 evangelists will win many to the Lord in this time of great hardship, evil and revival. The wicked will harden their hearts further, whilst many wavering sinners will be born again in a great spiritual awakening. Daniel said, 'Many shall be purified, made white and refined, but the wicked shall do wickedly; and none of the wicked shall understand, but the wise shall understand' " (Daniel 12:10).

"The countdown to the Apocalypse has begun," I said. "But why must there be so much destruction during the Tribulation?"

"The great war of Armageddon follows many judgments," replied the angel. "The Antichrist will send his global army to fight against Israel. He thinks he can stop God's plan. He believes he can destroy the seat of Christ's governance before the Millennial Reign, but he is deceived (Revelation 19:19-21).

"Satan has taken the nations captive, this is why they will give the Antichrist such power. In the natural realm, the Antichrist will focus on Israel being a troublesome country. He will argue they are the splinter in the Middle East. The 'problem' of the Third Jewish Temple will be paramount.

"The war will rage and a showdown will be reached at Megiddo, to the far north of Jerusalem. At Megiddo, at least twenty-one great battles have already taken place. Each one concerned what power will control the region.

"The Lord will return to earth at this point to fight for His people Israel. Satan's defeat will cause a thousand years of peace and abundance, when Christ will reign on earth. The Lord will speak His Word as He did at creation, and all the devastation of the Tribulation period, and all which preceded it, will be put right (Genesis 1:1, 26, John 1:1-3, Colossians 1:16, Hebrews 1:2, Revelation 4:11, 20:1-6).

"This new period of peace and prosperity during the Millennial Reign, will only be possible because the Lord will purge sin from earth. This is the reason for the Tribulation.

"God started again with Noah. He will start again with those who survive the Tribulation. It will be the last chance for earth and when Satan is released, some of mankind will choose him over the peace they experienced in the Millennial Reign. This will prepare the way for the new Heavens and a new earth in which righteousness dwells" (Revelation 20:7-10, 21:1-27).

"God will give people many chances," I said.

"When Storm Katrina flooded New Orleans in 2005, sin was silenced for a moment," said the angel. "What happened next? They did not fix the homes of the poor and vulnerable. The lowly were not considered first. But the dens of iniquity rushed to open. What does this tell you about mankind's priorities? Humanity will return to sin, as a dog returns to his vomit (Proverbs 26:11).

"Thus after the Tribulation, God will cleanse the world for a season. A new age of purity and beauty will unfold in the wonder which follows (Genesis 6:13, Matthew 24:37, Luke 11:50, Hebrews 11:7, 1 Peter 3:20).

"God is and always will be sovereign. In His sovereignty, He plans with the knowledge of what man will do. He gives humanity a free choice and He designs His will in anticipation of what they will choose. He knows they will spoil the Millennial Reign at the end, therefore He will create the new Heavens and earth with the Christ-nature of righteousness replacing the Adamic nature (Proverbs 16:4, Romans 9:17-24).

"Pharaoh was rebellious, but it was the Lord who raised him to be an example to every generation of God's power. Satan is not in charge and sin takes its course under the Lord's permissive will. The Almighty will allow people to reap what they have sown, to suffer at the consequences of their sin (Exodus 9:16, Jeremiah 19:5, Luke 7:30, Romans 1:28, 9:17).

"In and through all that happens, Jesus is Lord. It is only Jesus, the Alpha and the Omega, who is able to open the seal of the end times" (Revelation 5:1-5).

"Please show me one of these seals being broken," I asked.

I saw a small village in Asia. A man was cycling towards the local wet market and he bought a live animal, consuming it as he cycles. He is travelling to the airport where he works in a low paid job.

"He is host number one," said the angel.

As this man works as a baggage handler, he touches many cases and comes into close contact with other people. He's carrying an invisible infection. With an incubation period of four days, the infection spreads from this one man to many people in other airports. Flights travel around the world with the baggage containing the infection. All who touched these bags within three days received the invisible infection. With a four day incubation period, one man was able to spread the infection to thousands worldwide before they saw any symptoms.

"The fourth seal," said the angel. "One infection can lead to over two billion deaths! This is the pale horse carrying death through plagues and pandemics, leading to wars and hunger. It will cause huge numbers of the world's population to lose their lives" (Revelation 6:7-8).

"What a terrifying thought," I said.

"This is not the first time it has happened," said the angel. "In the fourteenth century, the Bubonic Plague killed up to fifty percent of Europe's population and close to twenty-five percent of the world's. It remains as the gravest biological disaster in recorded human history. The Black Death overwhelmed Europe, with healthy people in the morning dying the same day, discarding one in every two people to the grave! In 1918, the Spanish Flu killed up to one hundred million people; double those killed in the First World War!

"In the modern interconnected world, a few hosts can spread a deadly infection all over the planet in several days. Suddenly every hospital is flooded with patients. With healthcare systems overwhelmed, bodies will pileup in the streets. Covid-19 is mild compared to what is coming. The Great Plague of London from 1665 to 1666 killed almost a quarter of its population."

"There must be another way," I said again.

"In the redemptive plan of God, He will use this time of great trial to remove the altars mankind makes to money, wood and stone," said the angel.

"Hundreds of millions of people in India still worship

handmade idols and in the West, they put their trust in money and objects. Listen to Isaiah: 'For the Day of the Lord of hosts shall come upon everything proud and lofty, upon everything lifted up and it shall be brought low...in that day a man will cast away his idols of silver and his idols of gold, which they made, each for himself to worship, to the moles and bats, to go into the clefts of the rocks, and into the crags of the rugged rocks, from the terror of the Lord and the glory of His majesty, when He arises to shake the earth mightily' (Isaiah 2:12, 20-21).

"The Lord is coming for the whole world and everything must be shaken. When mankind learns it cannot trust in its own strength and idols, these will be thrown aside. They will then have a choice: Either submit to the true God in repentance and faith in Jesus Christ or harden one's heart to further destruction."

"In many nations that worship idols, Christians are persecuted," I said.

"Justice demands those who persecuted God's people will reap what they have sown, in double measure. Remember Jesus said, 'He sent out his armies and destroyed those murderers and burned up their city?' The spirit of judgment and the spirit of burning will satisfy the righteous judgment of God (Isaiah 4:4, Matthew 22:7).

"The world as you know it will end in God's perfect timing. Think of an age when volcanoes worldwide explode releasing sulphur oxides, dust and carbon dioxide, poisoning the land, falling with acid rain and inhibiting photosynthesis, leading to the collapse of the food chain."

"Unthinkable," I said.

"Think about signs from the Heavens, such as solar flares, supernovas and gamma rays, breaking down your communication systems, bursting the protection of the ozone layer, or the collapse of the magnetic field which defends earth from the worst the sun throws at it!"

Chapter Twenty

Antichrist Breaks the Treaty with Israel

"Despite the troubles of the first three and a half years of the Tribulation, the Antichrist will still enable the rich to prosper," said the angel, "just as the rich prospered during Covid-19, fleeing to safe havens of wealth. But the reign of the Antichrist will descend from problem solving before the seven years of the end times, to signing a peace treaty with Israel which commences the Tribulation and will end in extreme tyranny (Daniel 11:24).

"He will rise to power by respecting people of faith and will go to war with them later. National leaders who oppose him will be overthrown and emergency powers will become permanent. Think of Hitler in his bunker in Berlin, Germany, still dominating people and ruling by fear in 1945, as his capital city is collapsing.

"The Antichrist will masquerade as a peacemaker, as he forces Israel to negotiations about the status of Jerusalem and the Third Temple. As you have seen, Israel will be forced to sign a peace treaty dividing Jerusalem. Yet, when the moment is opportune, the Antichrist will find an advantage in breaking his treaty. The Temple will be invaded and sacrifices will be ended by force (Daniel 9:27).

"Soldiers from several nations will be chosen to attack Israel by the Antichrist," said the angel. "Muslim nations will be enraged by the site of the Third Temple. Watch out for Iran and Turkey leading Middle Eastern nations. Old alliances will draw Russia into the region and China has unlimited personnel (Revelation 9:16, 16:12).

"John prophesied: 'For they are spirits of demons, performing signs, which go out to the kings of the earth and of the whole world, to gather them to the battle of that great day of God Almighty' (Revelation 16:14).

"The Antichrist will break his peace treaty made with Israel due to satanic motivation and he will blame Israel.

He will manipulate the media to justify his devastation of the Holy Land. He will dispatch troops to overwhelm Israel and will appear to win quickly (Daniel 9:27).

"They will force the Jews to flee Jerusalem and other cities, but the Lord will give them supernatural protection. Some will find faith in Christ at this point, as they heed the preaching of the 144,000 (Ezekiel 16:8-14, Micah 4:10, Revelation 12:6, 13-16).

"Filled with rage for all the problems he thinks religious people are causing him, Antichrist will ultimately engage in a war of totality against all people of faith. He will begin with Jews and Christians (Daniel 11:36-39, 2 Thessalonians 2:3-4, Revelation 12:17).

"When the Jews are forced to flee, this will signal the beginning of the second half of the Tribulation, with greater judgments following. Jesus imparted this wisdom to the Jews of the end times: 'Then let those who are in Judea flee to the mountains. Let him who is on the housetop not go down to take anything out of his house...and pray that your flight may not be in winter or on the Sabbath. For then there will be Great Tribulation, such as has not been since the beginning of the world until this time, no, nor ever shall be' (Matthew 24:16-21).

"Did you notice Jesus predicted events are not fixed because prayer can change them? If supplication couldn't change end time seasons, the Lord would not have said, 'Pray that your flight may not be in winter or on the Sabbath.'

"The nation you know as Jordan will resist the Antichrist and many Jews will flee to their neighbour and receive safe passage. When Jesus said, 'Flee to the mountains,' those who heard Him understood the historic reference of escaping to safety in the mountains in the nation you now call Jordan. In this wilderness, they will seek God for a revelation about their Messiah-King. John saw this: 'Then the woman fled into the wilderness, where she has a place prepared by God, that they should feed her there one thousand two hundred and sixty days' " (Isaiah 16:4, Ezekiel 20:35-36, Revelation 12:6).

"I expect evangelicals will also stand with God's chosen people at this time," I said.

"Not if evangelicals are being persecuted," replied the angel.

I watched a special address being given by the President of the Union on a large screen. He was arrayed immaculately and spoke with calm assurance, "My fellow citizens," said Antichrist, "at this moment Union forces are in the foundational stages of military operations to disarm Israel. Our struggle is not with Israeli citizens, but with the illegal actions of its leadership. The goal of our forces is to free the people of Israel and the territories from a rogue government, and to liberate the Temple Mount.

"To the fighting men and women who cross into Israel today, the Union is looking to you to bring tranquillity to a troubled region. Our forces will restore peace to the Middle East and dissolve a deepening crisis.

"Having consulted the ten leaders of our Union, we have committed to securing peace in the region. Our peacekeepers will enter the Temple in the spirit of neutrality and brotherhood, end this bloodlust and find a peaceful settlement with Muslim leaders.

"For this reason, I have authorised our peacekeepers to bring about a peaceful transition of power from this Israeli regime. We will establish a new transitional government that will work in harmony with the Union to address global concerns.

"I now order all Israeli military units to lay down arms and welcome our peacekeepers. If we meet resistance, all the military power of our Union will be brought to bear upon the Israeli occupation forces.

"I urge the government of Israel to immediately surrender to Union representatives in our embassies. If you order troops to fight us, we will hold you accountable under international law.

"We remain at heart a peaceful Union, but our hands have been forced. Union peacekeepers, stationed in bases in Iraq, Iran and Syria, and in the region, have already been authorised to begin their move toward Israel. Our peacekeepers will bring an end to the illegal occupation, free the Temple Mount and defuse this great threat to peace in our world."

"This is it," I exclaimed, "Armageddon!"

As I spoke these words, Israel's prime minister gave an address to the media, as sirens sounded in Israel. Troops were mobilised and a state of war declared. The prime minister said, "Israel is a sovereign state and will defend itself," and concluded a succinct statement by saying, "No options are off the table."

The war was vicious. Israel is an advanced military power, but it could not contend with the latest technology from a global supply chain. Israel was forced to launch five or six nuclear weapons on Middle Eastern bases. I expected a nuclear apocalypse, but Israeli systems were hacked and launch sites jammed.

Tanks, planes, drones, boats and personnel overwhelmed Israeli borders from every direction. Israeli forces withdrew at the overwhelming numbers and fell back into a slither of their land. Jewish citizens ran for their lives and every road was covered with people and vehicles trying to find somewhere to flee.

Unprecedented numbers of civilians were killed, as an army which seems without number overpowered Israel. Soon the Temple Mount was seized.

"With the taking of the Temple Mount, the last hindrance to Antichrist is overcome," said the angel. "The pretender Man of Peace will become at war with all. All who oppose Antichrist will be attacked and all remaining unconforming politicians arrested. All people of faith will suffer. All contenders will be crushed under his might.

"The Antichrist will go mad under demonic possession and will believe he is god. Nothing he has sought to achieve has failed. All is under his power. This is the beginning of the nightmare of the second three and a half years of Tribulation" (Daniel 7:25, 12:7, Revelation 11:3, 12:6, 12:14, 13:5).

Chapter Twenty-One

The Abomination of Desolation

"The Bible says Antichrist will not regard the faith of his fathers," I said. "Does this mean he comes from a Christian or Jewish family?"

"John tells you all you need to know," said the angel. "Who is a liar, but he who denies that Jesus is the Christ? He is antichrist who denies the Father and the Son. Whoever denies the Son does not have the Father either; he who acknowledges the Son has the Father also" (1 John 2:22-23).

"I wonder what this signifies," I said.

"Anyone who does not acknowledge Jesus Christ in all His fullness, as revealed in the Word of God, is under the power of the spirit of antichrist. Everyone who prays and worships 'a god,' who does not recognise Jesus Christ is empowering the antichrist spirit. They are praying to demonic spirits, and they are feeding on their prayers and declarations.

"When Christians intercede in the Holy Spirit, demonic powers are weakened. But people praying to other gods empower the demonic. Heed John: 'Every spirit that does not confess that Jesus Christ has come in the flesh is not of God. And this is the spirit of the Antichrist, which you have heard was coming, and is now already in the world'" (1 John 4:3).

"What does it convey when it says 'Jesus Christ has come in the flesh?' " I asked.

"The incarnation in all its fullness," he replied. "Because Jesus is the Way, the Truth and the Life, and the Alpha and Omega, the enemy's attack is focused upon Jesus being the Son of God. Jesus is equal with the Father. God in Christ came to earth to put on human flesh and became man (John 5:23, 10:30-33, 14:9-11, 17:5).

"Jesus existed before the foundation of the world. He came from Heaven. Therefore, He was eternally alive before Abraham, the founder of the faith. Both Abraham and Moses looked to Jesus" (John 5:39, 6:41-42, 8:56-58, 17:24).

"I have heard it said the Abomination of Desolation, referenced by Daniel and Jesus is the Dome of the Rock in Jerusalem," I stated. "This Muslim shrine has a text around it declaring God has no Son. Many believe this building now stands exactly where the Jewish Temple once stood" (Daniel 9:27, 11:31, 12:11, Mark 13:14).

"As with most prophecies in Scripture, there is more than one fulfilment," he replied. "Any attack on the revelation of Jesus Christ represents an abomination. However, the Abomination of Desolation contains a specific revelation concerning the termination of sacrifices in the Temple of Jerusalem in the end times; yet it may not be fulfilled as you expect.

"The Lord moves through the shadows of time. Events are not fixed; one Holy Spirit awakening can delay Antichrist. God works with humanity and He advances His plans based upon their obedience" (Exodus 32:14, Numbers 14:34, 2 Samuel 24:16, Jeremiah 26:3, Isaiah 38:4-5, Jonah 3:9, Amos 7:3, 2 Peter 3:12).

"When was the first fulfilment of the abomination prophecy?" I asked.

"In 165 BC, a Greek ruler called Antiochus IV annulled the biblical sacrifices in Jerusalem and slaughtered a pig on the altar of the Temple of God. This was the first Abomination of Desolation. Jesus predicted the second abomination concerning the future defilement of the Temple by the Romans, making it desolate in AD 70 (Luke 21:5-7, 20-22).

"The third Abomination of Desolation will be revealed in the last days. Jesus spoke of it in the Gospels and Ezekiel spoke of a 'Seat of Jealously.' This is the seat of the Antichrist residing in the Third Jewish Temple after his armies have occupied Jerusalem (Ezekiel 8:3, Matthew 24:16, Mark 13:14).

"This third desolation of the Temple is the revelation of the Man of Sin – notice he is a man – attempting to seat himself in the place of God in the Temple, as the world ruler. Only Jesus can rule and reign in the nations from

Jerusalem (Isaiah 14:12-15, Ezekiel 28:12-17).

"When first century Christians feared they missed the return of Jesus, Paul gave them this wisdom: 'Let no one deceive you by any means; for that Day – the return of Christ – will not come unless the falling away comes first, and the Man of Sin is revealed, the Son of Perdition, who opposes and exalts himself above all that is called God or that is worshipped, so that he sits as God in the Temple of God, showing himself that he is God' " (2 Thessalonians 2:3-4).

A reporter was filming from the steps of the Temple in Jerusalem. She identified as 'progressive' and blamed the Jews for the wars in the Middle East. She alleged the recent problems started with the building of the Third Temple on the site where the Dome of the Rock once stood. She said it was cruel for animals to be sacrificed in the Temple and praised the President of the Union for diffusing the chaos in Jerusalem. She declared the holy city was fully under Union control and all of Israel will be quickly restored to peace by the Union military."

"Biased," I said, shaking my head.

The angel replied, "And from the time that the daily sacrifice is taken away, and the Abomination of Desolation is set up, there shall be one thousand two hundred and ninety days" (Daniel 12:11).

A statement from the President of the Union followed the report: "This Temple has been at the centre of the conflict tearing apart the Middle East," said Antichrist. "Now liberated, it will become a symbol of peace and stability. Our Union fought to liberate the Temple Mount and our united world has restored peace to Jerusalem; it will deliver peace to Israel.

"In preparation to negotiate an ongoing peaceful settlement for this holy city, this Union has decided to establish a temporal government office inside the Temple. I have been asked by leaders of the ten regions to personally officiate over the Office of Peace to be established in the Temple. This will be a temporal office, until we find a lasting peace."

"Those who do wickedly against the covenant he shall corrupt with flattery," said the angel. "The time of trouble for the Jews has just begun. They have been driven from Jerusalem and will be forced to retreat all over Israel, but the Lord will rescue them in due time (Daniel 11:32).

"Think once more on the words of Jesus, 'Therefore when you see the Abomination of Desolation, spoken of by Daniel the prophet, standing in the holy place, then let those who are in Judea flee to the mountains...for then there will be Great Tribulation, such as has not been since the beginning of the world until this time, no, nor ever shall be. And unless those days were shortened, no flesh would be saved; but for the elect's sake those days will be shortened' " (Matthew 24:15-22).

As the Jews fled throughout Israel, God provided them with supernatural protection on a slither of land. Those who could hide in the rocks, caves and deserts did. Others retreated into underground bunkers. As the war progressed, the Antichrist made no distinction between soldiers and civilians, as many were killed or imprisoned (Revelation 12:14-17).

"I once assumed the Antichrist was a religious man," I said. "At the moment he seems like a devious politician."

"The enemy is slyer than you can imagine," I was told. "He has learnt he cannot succeed with a glaring deception. He always works in the shadows. Which of the disciples realised Judas was the enemy within? Jesus called Judas the Son of Perdition and Paul used the same name to identify the Antichrist. If Satan can enter Judas, he can enter Antichrist too (Luke 22:3, John 13:27, 17:12, 2 Thessalonians 2:3).

"If the Man of Sin was obvious, believers would not fall for the deception. The enemy must give people as much room as possible to doubt their fears. The Son of Perdition will oppose and exalt himself above all that is called God. He will sit in the Temple of God, but first he must win their approval. Think about it! The media does not call violent rioters and looters criminals, if they are considered to be on the 'right side of history.' There is a double standard applied to those who call themselves by the right name" (Matthew 24:24-25, 2 Thessalonians 2:3-4).

We saw Jerusalem again. The Antichrist emerged from

the Temple standing on the steps before a cheering crowd. They shouted in hypnotic chants. Religious leaders stood in the crowd weeping and clapping the man whom they believed would create a lasting peace in Jerusalem. Those who lived in fear and lack praised the Antichrist for restoring some order and providing supplies amid an unfolding nightmare.

"They make him out to be a god," the angel said. "They claim to worship God, but deep in their heart they have enthroned Antichrist as their provider. In their soul, God is dethroned and the Son of Perdition is the one they believe will save them from chaos. Even religious Christians are praying for his success and God's blessing upon him" (Proverbs 17:3, Matthew 15:8).

"What must the Lord think?" I said.

"The Lord is in control," said the angel. "As disasters overtake the world and humbles it, God will watch and test people's hearts. But in the end, the Lord will give them what they want, sending 'them a strong delusion, that they should believe the lie' (Deuteronomy 8:2, 2 Thessalonians 2:11).

"As the peoples of the world place their faith in this man, in praise and honour, they choose deception. As the Antichrist has control over a mighty military machine, no one can defeat him in war. In the Heavenly realms praise of this man will become an act of worship. Listen to John: 'So they worshipped the dragon who gave authority to the Beast; and they worshipped the Beast, saying, 'Who is like the Beast? Who is able to make war with him?' (Revelation 13:4).

"When they set their hope in Antichrist, they are in fact worshipping Satan and his plan for a counterfeit Millennial Reign. This is the reason why the deception is finely tuned, so you can't recognise it. Liberty ends with people clapping, shouting and hypnotically chanting" (John 8:44, 1 John 3:8-10).

"How deep will the deception go?" I asked.

"Satan will begin with what is palatable. He couldn't introduce abortion by showing people a fully grown baby being torn apart. He started with the idea of a very small number of cells that needs removing. These cells were called a foetus. Then a fully grown baby was called a foetus. Little by little the deception unfolds and the boundaries move.

"When people have accepted Antichrist as a secular leader, he will move into the supernatural of the demonic. Jesus walked on water, commanded the weather, healed the sick and raised the dead. Satan always tries to counterfeit God's work. Therefore, a paradigm shift in thinking will unfold as Antichrist and his evil trinity moves in demonic supernatural power. The Antichrist will elevate another who is to become the Second Beast, in an unholy trinity of rebellion against God" (Revelation 13:11-18).

"Another man!" I exclaimed.

"When the Antichrist reveals his true colours and the world witnesses supernatural power working through him for their apparent betterment, they will idolise him more. But it is not him they truly love; it is Satan working through him. They have rejected the Son of Man, so they get the Son of Perdition.

"When the alleged Man of Peace is fully in power, he will give himself over to Satan in totality. The devil will empower him and he will be worshipped as a god.

"Heed this warning: In the last times, there will be an unholy demonic trinity of Satan, the Antichrist and the False Prophet. All that is anti-God, anti-Christ and anti-Israel will be enshrined within them. This spirit is already at work in the world today, rejecting Christ, despising God, hating Israel and boycotting their goods. Those who oppose the Antichrist's attack on Israel will be outlaws."

Chapter Twenty-Two

A Counterfeit Resurrection

Several weeks passed and a magnificent funeral was being prepared. A coffin sat in the middle of a square and hundreds of thousands of people queued to pay their respects. The body of a man was inside an open coffin and his face was visible for all to see. It was the President of the Union, the Antichrist (Revelation 13:3).

"Three days ago, a lone Jewish sniper shot and killed the President as he was leaving the Temple complex in Jerusalem," said a reporter, with sleepless eyes. "This was a shameful assault made on our fragile peace. The motivation of the assassin is unknown; but many believe he was a religious extremist seeking revenge for the temporary seizure of the Temple.

"World leaders have responded calling for calm. They are determined we will not be driven off course. We will not be intimidated. Thugs, mobs and threats will not keep us from our peaceful goals.

"Our President understood the danger of entering Jerusalem before peace was fully restored and he accepted this risk for all of mankind. Medical experts from around the world fought for his life and after hours of struggle, they verified his sad passing. Never has the medical profession fought to save one life with such intensity.

"The President, knowing the risk, stated if anything should happen to him, he wanted to be remembered as a martyr for peace. In his will, he ordered his body should be displayed on all media outlets for all the world to see, to teach the nations that 'violence begets violence.' We warn you that some viewers may be shocked by what we are about to broadcast."

The corpse of the President of the Union was shown by the media. I questioned the images. Was the Antichrist dead or just wounded? (2 Thessalonians 2:11).

The reporter saw a mourner near the open coffin and the lady spoke of her sadness, saying the President was her martyr. "He gave his life to prove through sacrifice, we can rebuild our nations in peace," she said. "Religion has torn us apart, but his death has united us in peace."

The coffin was unusually open, and a mourner evaded the gaze of security and fell on the body weeping. "He's so cold," said the mourner, as the guards failed to intervene. "Look at his face, it's grey. He's our Abraham Lincoln, our JFK. He is Camelot, our King Arthur. The Man of Peace is dead, the one called to lead us into a golden age of hope."

I questioned why this person was allowed access to the Antichrist's body and why everything she said was broadcast. The guards ushered her on and she held out her hand, gliding along his body, craving the last touch. Then, as her hand reached his foot, his body jerked. An earth tremor then knocked the crowd off balance and a hand reached out of the coffin, to touch the woman. The lady screamed; first in horror, followed by tears and she cried out, "He's alive, He's alive, He's come back from the dead!"

The guards appeared panic stricken. The crowd rushed forwards in confusion and swamped the coffin. TV cameras captured them moving forward to the casket with their hands stretched toward it. Suddenly the people all bowed in unison onto their knees. Rising amongst them from his coffin was the Antichrist, the President of the Union.

"Staged," I said, in cynical mistrust.

The Antichrist stepped down from the coffin and walked amongst the people stooped before him. He glided through the silent crowds without saying a word, touching those with bowed heads. A security team moved towards him slowly and after five minutes of calm ushered him away.

The world was silent. Every system of communication was replaying the scenes. A few hours passed and a medical expert was speaking in a studio, with a number of celebrities agreeing with him.

"I was brought up to be a cynic," he said, "and my

professionalism leads me to approach everything with deep scepticism. I can't explain what happened. The best doctors in the world tried to save our President and he died. He was declared dead. I know these doctors, they're not tinpots, they're the best. No one can survive the wound inflicted upon him without a miracle.

"He's the first man to come back from the dead and show himself openly as resurrected. I don't know if you believe in God, I certainly don't. But maybe if He is real, He performed a miracle yesterday. Our President is back to bring peace to this deeply troubled world. We are living in an age of miracles!"

The scene of the Antichrist rising out of his coffin was repeated continually until every screen in the nations went blank. The following words flashed onto every device worldwide: 'Standby for a special address by the President of the Union.'

After a few minutes, the President appeared on people's screens, sitting behind a table inside the Third Temple, with the symbols of power behind him. "I came to give my life for you," said the Antichrist, with a lengthy pause, "for peace." The sound of clapping was heard on the streets of the world.

"Three days ago I was shot and you saw my dead body. Hate killed me; bigotry slayed me. Blind faith executed me! But behold, I am he who was dead and now I am alive forevermore!"

The sound of the crowd's shouting could be heard echoing in the chambers of the Temple. "You came to see me to pay your respects," he said, "and now I return to pay respect to you."

I heard people chanting words of praise and adoration.

"When I died, I was taken into another realm and met the prince of the power of the air. He is our god; the god of this world. He said I was chosen to be the first to be raised from the dead. He showed me the kingdoms of this world and gave them to me, and now I give them back to you (Matthew 4:8-11, 2 Corinthians 4:4, Ephesians 2:2).

"The religions of this world have not delivered peace, but division. I have returned to heal the divide; to be the bridge between life and death. I will show you the way, for I have walked the path of death to life for you."

With each statement people cheered, chanted and praised. The Antichrist spoke slowly with thought, giving people time to think and respond to each sentence.

"The noble spirit who spoke to me told me I was to return to life with new power," said Antichrist. "Power to aid those with no hope; power to heal the sick. Power to change the weather, stop meteorites and calm earthquakes. I am your servant, sent back to save you from this hour of trouble."

"What!" I quipped.

"Many cynics do not believe in such power," he said. "Let them promptly come to the porch outside of this great Temple and witness this power at work in me. I will bring peace to this world by strength. I will heal the sick. Death will flee at my power. Let all who cannot be cured with medicine come to the Temple and I will heal them as a sign of my power."

The Antichrist walked outside of the Temple into a crowd that was gathering. Everything was broadcast live to the nations. He laid his hands on the lame, blind and sick. All became well. People wept and claimed they never felt such joy before. Someone in the crowd shouted, "The voice of a god and not of a man" (Acts 12:22).

"This must be a trick," I said to the angel.

"He is the counterfeit messiah," the angel said. "The Antichrist copies everything the true Messiah has accomplished. This man heals the sick by evil power because Christ healed the sick by God's power and he speaks of love, as Christ did" (Matthew 4:23-25).

"How can this power be available to him?" I asked.

"He is the servant of Satan, the dragon and he has given him the power. John prophesied of the 'mortally wounded' being healed and the world following him. Read the Word of God again and open your eyes: 'The dragon gave him his power, his throne and great authority. And I saw one of his heads as if it had been mortally wounded, and his deadly wound was healed. And all the world marvelled and followed the Beast. So they worshipped the dragon who gave authority to the Beast; and they worshipped the Beast, saying, 'Who is like the Beast? Who is able to make war with him?' " (Revelation 13:2-4).

"I don't understand why God would allow such power to be released by Satan," I said, "because millions will perish in this deceit."

"Paul said this: 'The coming of the Lawless One is according to the working of Satan, with all power, signs and lying wonders, and with all unrighteous deception among those who perish, because they did not receive the love of the truth, that they might be saved. And for this reason God will send them a strong delusion, that they should believe the lie, that they all may be condemned who did not believe the truth but had pleasure in unrighteousness' " (2 Thessalonians 2:9-12).

Chapter Twenty-Three

The Beast from the Earth

A few days passed and a press conference was called. The world's media was prepped to broadcast Antichrist's message, unchallenged. The President of the Union appeared in front of the Third Temple speaking to the nations, "My fellow citizens," he said, "we do not live in days of peace, but we hope for peace. All over the world there are churches and synagogues. But where is the peace they promised?

"In the nations I see extremism, hatred and division. Christianity and Judaism have had centuries to secure peace, but it never came. They brought war and division. They compelled us to focus on what separates us, rather than what unites.

"Religious faith has become a poison driving us apart. It has drained the life from this world. When Christians and Jews pray, these prayers go towards a spiritual power which has caused the calamity that has come upon us.

"In the cause of peace, I speak to all nations. Enough is enough! From this day forth, I announce an emergency degree to keep all houses of worship closed until we purge those who preach bigotry from our midst. I have ordered troops to seize all religious leaders who preach division and secure their buildings. It is for peace I now act."

"Churches will be closed!" I exclaimed, in consternation.

"It is prophesied," said the angel. "And he was given a mouth speaking great things and blasphemies, and he was given authority to continue for forty-two months. Then he opened his mouth in blasphemy against God, to blaspheme His name, His tabernacle and those who dwell in Heaven. It was granted to him to make war with the saints and to overcome them. And authority was given him over every tribe, tongue and nation. All who dwell on the earth will worship him, whose names have not been written in the *Book of Life* of the Lamb slain from the foundation of the world" (Revelation 13:2-8).

"Christians have told us they serve a God of power," continued the Antichrist. "But where is the power to save us from these terrible days? Where is the help from this kind, merciful and benevolent God? Preachers tell us to repent and claim we are subject to the wrath of the Almighty; not a merciful God then. Meanwhile, our homes burn, our cities crumble and our loved ones die and He does not reply."

In the spiritual world, demonic spirits manifested and unlocked the hearts of the sinful to heed the Antichrist (Daniel 10:12-14, Ephesians 6:12).

"If the God of the Bible possesses no power to help," said Antichrist, "then we will ask another. I speak of the spirit who raised me from the dead and granted me supernatural power to help others."

A man presently walked from the Third Temple and stood by the Antichrist, and this man was given the title the Global Minister for Religious Affairs. "Before my death, I was always a man of science and logic," said Antichrist. "I never believed in supernatural power and yet the spirit beyond death opened my eyes. As my heart was laid bare to the supernatural world, I have been sent to open yours too.

"The spirit who brought me back from the dead conferred power on me and I impart this anointing to the Global Minister of Religious Affairs. He is the One; the One chosen to be a channel for the power of the spirit beyond death. He is the One anointed by me to save you."

"He's gone mad," I overheard people say quietly in their homes.

"To those who mock my words I say open your eyes and see," said Antichrist. "The One will save you with my power. The One will deliver you. There is no need to pray to Heaven for help anymore. Heaven is silent but the One will save us."

"A lunatic is in charge of the world," said a listener to himself in the quiet of his home.

The Antichrist and the One paced on the Temple Mount

in Jerusalem and the former said, "Look up to the sky."

A small meteorite was falling towards Jerusalem and the people fled, but the guards forced them to stay in a sizeable crowd. The Antichrist turned to the One and said, "Raise your hands," and he did. "Now speak to the meteorite and command fire to come down from the Heavens to disintegrate it!"

A satanic cry came from the mouth of the One commanding fire to fall and suddenly it tumbled from the sky, raining down towards earth and burnt up the meteorite. The crowds cheered and the world watched in awe.

"A shabby media trick," said a viewer watching at home.

"I hear your voice," said Antichrist, "a shabby media trick!" The man who said these words sat up in horror. "To prove to all this power is real, the power to save you from terror, I urge all to go outside of your homes and see with the naked eye. This miracle will take place all over the world to prove your saviour has come. The One will save us and the One will serve me."

The people of earth left their homes or tents and stood outside looking up. Cynicism was deep but the Tribulation devastated people's lives and they were primed to believe anything from the Antichrist, if it offered hope. Next, tiny meteorites fell from the Heavens all over and fire from the One dissolved them. People sensed only burning ash and the smell of sulphur.

"It's too hard to believe," I said.

"Listen to the Word of God again," said the angel. "And he exercises all the authority of the first Beast in his presence, and causes the earth and those who dwell in it to worship the first Beast, whose deadly wound was healed. He performs great signs, so that he even makes fire come down from Heaven on the earth in the sight of men" (Revelation 13:12-13).

"I don't understand," I cried out. "Is God in control or not?"

"The Scriptures remain your sole guide," said the angel, "and contemporary translations try to find further meaning from the original language: 'The coming of the Lawless One will be in accordance with how Satan works. He will use all sorts of displays of power through signs and wonders that serve the lie, and all the ways that wickedness deceives those who are perishing. They perish because they refused to love the truth and be saved. For this reason God sends them a powerful delusion, so that they will believe the lie and so that all will be condemned who have not believed the truth but have delighted in wickedness' " (2 Thessalonians 2:9-12).

"It's all a lie," I said.

Time passed and the Antichrist with the One exercised an iron fist rule over the world. The man called the One by Antichrist, I knew to be the Second Beast in the Bible (Revelation 13:11-16).

Thick dust clouds engulfed parts of the world after volcanoes burst and meteorites struck. But now by the command of the One, the thick dust was parted. He exercised demonic authority over nature and it was bent to his will. Just as Christ displayed mastery over nature, so the counterfeit will move in power to deceive many (Mark 4:35-41, Revelation 13:13).

A broadcast debate was taking place about the power of the President and the One: "Clearly, we support the President," said an expert, pretending to be objective in a media which was controlled by the Antichrist. "For he is restoring order to our troubled world, but as a scientist, I must stress I don't believe in the supernatural. I believe they have access to some super technology, perhaps from an alien source, which they use to protect us. We are begotten of stardust after all."

"Who cares how," contested a celebrity. "These two leaders are liberating us from the power of nature. They offer us hope in a time of hopelessness. We prayed and nothing happened; now we are seeing real change."

Another expert leaned forward to speak, "As a scientist, I think there is evidence that the One is leading us forward into a new stage of human evolution. He has demonstrated that humans can connect with the spiritual world. It is a known fact there are parts of our brain that remain dormant. Conceivably all of us can learn to exercise the dormant parts of our brain to control things outside of ourselves."

A New Age spokesperson announced, "For thousands of years our ancestors believed in magic and supernatural power. In our pride we thought they were wrong. But because of the President and the One, we have had a paradigm shift. Our eyes have been opened to the spiritual world – to supernatural power. There is more to this world than the natural order. We are spiritual beings. This is a brave new world beyond science and into the supernatural."

A vicar was present, one who made a deal with the Antichrist system and he said, "Many like me are believers in God and I think the Almighty sent these two men to deliver us. If Jesus was here, I believe He would embrace the President and the One.

"As a supernaturalist," said the compromised vicar, "I believe interferences can take place in our universe from other systems outside of it. We may call it god or a higher power, or an alien. The point is we are seeing it. Someone is helping us. Our understanding of science and the supernatural is limited.

"Many religious extremists are resisting the Union," said the vicar. "I believe God sent the President and the One to aid us in these troubled times. I urge all Christians, Jews, Muslims and all religious people to support these men. I urge all to accept the identity technology on your right hand or forehead. As long as we can detect you, we can help. If the police come to your house to arrest you, tell them, 'We pledge allegiance to the President and the One,' and they will upgrade your Identification Mark to safe.

"Regrettably, the former norms of the rule of law cannot be followed in this crisis. But there is no need for anyone to suffer under a mistaken arrest. Big government will provide for you; this is why we rely on your declaration of faith in the government. Please, perform your civic duty and support it. We should bestow honour where honour is due, that's in the Bible. The President 'is God's minister to you for good' " (Romans 13:4, 7).

Chapter Twenty-Four

Two Supernatural Witnesses

With all the world's power under his jurisdiction, the Antichrist with the Beast unveiled a reign of terror against the true people of faith. Daniel said, "I was watching and the same horn was making war against the saints and prevailing against them" (Daniel 7:21-22).

For decades the biased media provoked resentment against Christians and now its attacks were upfront. Jesus said, "Then they will deliver you up to tribulation and kill you, and you will be hated by all nations for My name's sake. And then many will be offended, will betray one another, and will hate one another" (Matthew 24:9-10).

I saw genuine Christian leaders and their prophets speaking against Antichrist and warning of the disasters to follow, but people just laughed, saying, "A broken clock is right twice a day."

"The prophets of the Lord have spoken," said the angel, "but the people will not heed them. To the secular-minded they are mere humans. They dissect the words of the prophets, twisting them to their advantage. For this reason, the Lord will send two supernatural witnesses whom the world cannot ignore!"

The global media was focused upon Jerusalem. Then out of the sky approached a white light and two supernatural people appeared, in bodies of flesh and blood. Journalists speculated that they could be representatives of an alien species and asked why they had come.

"I think I know who they are," I said, "Elijah and Moses."

The angel did not confirm or deny my conclusion. The two witnesses pronounced judgment on the nations, prophesying and calling the world to repentance. Many days passed and the Antichrist ordered them to be arrested.

When Union forces approached them, they found they possessed no power over them. When they advanced they could not press through an invisible shield of Divine power. They discharged shots at the two witnesses to no avail. The bullets could not come near them. The two witnesses spoke the Word of God, and fire came from their mouths and killed those who ambushed them.

"The world is not familiar with this kind of supernatural manifestation," I said.

The area was secured and journalists stood nearby to report these undertakings. "Representatives from the Union have stated they are monitoring the situation," said one broadcaster. "This area of Jerusalem will remain sealed to the public, as a safety precaution. We are being warned not to heed the message of these two beings. This is not a time for division but unity."

"God will empower the two witnesses to speak for forty-two months," said the angel. "This represents the second half of the Tribulation period, which lasts for three and a half years. When the nations refuse to repent, they will prophesy and rain will not fall. When they declare the waters will turn to blood, it shall be performed. Plagues will descend on their command. The fulfilment of their prophecies will be exact, so no one can claim they are false prophets.

"Listen to the Bible," continued the angel. " 'I will give power to my two witnesses, and they will prophesy one thousand two hundred and sixty days, clothed in sackcloth.' These are the two olive trees and the two lamp stands standing before the God of the earth. And if anyone wants to harm them, fire proceeds from their mouth and devours their enemies. And if anyone wants to harm them, he must be killed in this manner. These have power to shut Heaven, so that no rain falls in the days of their prophecy; and they have power over waters to turn them to blood, and to strike the earth with all plagues, as often as they desire" (Revelation 11:3-6).

"Elijah called down fire from Heaven and Moses commanded the waters to turn to blood," I said. "These must be the two anointed ones, who stand beside the Lord of the whole earth" (Zechariah 4:14).

"But Enoch and Elijah never died," said the angel (Genesis 5:24, 2 Kings 2:1).

The two witnesses appeared during the ongoing war against Israel. Jerusalem had fallen, Israel had not.

"Hate is rising against the Jewish people," replied the angel. "The Antichrist forces will move on from seeking the occupation of Israel to planning the annihilation of the Jews in the Holy Land."

"No!" I said.

"It has happened several times before from Bible times to the Holocaust," said the angel. "Satan hates the Jews and he will stir up hatred against Israel."

"Will Antichrist forces really obey him and try to commit this genocide?" I asked.

"The bitter truth of history is that any government who wanted to annihilate their enemies without or within, has never failed to find a shortage of willing executioners," said the angel. "Communists, such as Stalin and Mao killed over one hundred million people through death camps, wars, gulags, or failed economic policies.

"Each dictator in history has found a supply of soldiers, doctors, lawyers and politicians ready to brutalise and kill for a living. They dehumanise their enemy first and construct an organised framework of conformity, where powerful people rise to the occasion of death.

"To bolster their case, the dictator sells their crimes as self-defence and righting a wrong, to drawdown resistance. Even Adolf Hitler found his experts, lawyers, doctors, soldiers and politicians to execute his nefarious deeds. Wherever there's a Hitler, there's a Himmler, Eichmann, Göring, Eicke and Höss, all ready to kill in his name.

"This is why Christian resistance to this profane world must remain strong. As long as believers are openly resisting, questioning and saying, 'No,' the enemy can be restrained (2 Thessalonians 2:6-8).

"An entire generation of silent German Christians allowed the Nazis to take control. Few remember it was in the Garrison Church or Garnisonkirche, on 23 March 1933, where Hitler became 'spiritually' legitimised before Germany's elite. The backslidden Church will welcome the Antichrist when he comes, just as the German Church welcomed Hitler.

"People forget their history. Hitler came to power through the popular vote. He manipulated the polling system. Then, in the parliamentary election and referendum of 10 April 1938, turnout in the election was officially 99.5% with 98.9% voting 'yes' to Hitler.

"Only Heaven knows the names of the few who voted 'No.' If you were alive in Germany in this time, would you have voted against Hitler? If you are submissive to this world and conforming to their standards, you would have submitted then. Many think they would have resisted, but when Hitler promised help in testing times, people chose him. Are you a conforming parrot, repeating what 'they' say you should say, or are you a disciple of the Way, the Truth and the Life?

"Just as Germany rejected the good and chose an antichrist figure in Hitler, so the nations will reject the warnings of the two supernatural witnesses and follow the Antichrist.

"Listen to the Bible: 'When the two witnesses finished their testimony, the Beast that ascends out of the bottomless pit will make war against them, overcome them and kill them. And their dead bodies will lie in the street of the great city which spiritually is called Sodom and Egypt, where also our Lord was crucified. Then those from the peoples, tribes, tongues, and nations will see their dead bodies three and a half days, and not allow their dead bodies to be put into graves. And those who dwell on the earth will rejoice over them, make merry, and send gifts to one another because these two prophets tormented those who dwell on the earth. Now after the three and a half days the breath of life from God entered them, and they stood on their feet, and great fear fell on those who saw them. And they heard a loud voice from Heaven saying to them, 'Come up here.' And they ascended to Heaven in a cloud, and their enemies saw them' " (Revelation 11:7-12).

"Do you comprehend what this signifies?" asked the angel.

"No."

"There are several Raptures in the Bible," he replied. "The Greek word for Rapture written in English letters is 'harpazo.' It means 'to snatch, to grab, to pull up.'

1. "Enoch was taken (Genesis 5:23-24; Hebrews 11:5)

2. "Elijah was snatched in a whirlwind (2 Kings 2:11).

3. "Jesus ascended into Heaven (Acts 1:9-11).

4. "The Church will be Raptured before the Tribulation (1 Thessalonians 4:15-16).

5. "The two supernatural witnesses will be pulled into Heaven during the Tribulation (Revelation 11:11-12).

"There will also be two great reapings in this season:

1. "The earth will be reaped of those saved during the first half of the Tribulation (Revelation 14:14-16).

2. "The damned of Armageddon will be harvested for judgment" (Revelation 14:17-20).

"It will be a wonder to behold," I exclaimed.

"Then Babylon must fall," said the angel. "The Babylon of the last days is the world system of commerce and idolatry. Babylon and Rome were at the heart of trading empires and religious idolatry. Thus, all which keeps mankind from Christ will collapse. The love of money, abundance and luxury will end. The embrace of the demonic media will end. Death, mourning and famine will replace lust, sinful celebration and obese wealth (Revelation 18:1-24).

"The fall of Babylon will lead to the end of the Gentile grip on political and financial power. For the first time since Solomon, Israel will rise to become the world's greatest nation, with Christ as the King of the Messianic age. Israel, though small, will be the centre of a global empire, just like Great Britain was. It will be a reign of peace and satisfaction. The world will own fewer goods but will find true treasure in Jesus Christ."

Chapter Twenty-Five

A Mountain Falls from the Sky

"You must appreciate the events you are being shown will take place during the Tribulation period," said the angel. "The signs of seven will take place in conjunction with all the other events, including the prophesying of the two supernatural witnesses. Their declarations will coincide with events described in the coming time of sorrows, with the seven seals, trumpets, secret thunders and bowls of wrath."

"Ok," I acknowledged.

"In the solar system there are countless numbers of rogue objects orbiting the sun. By the grace of God's plan in creation, they do not strike earth; a perfect balance has been created to drag these objects away from earth. This balance will be smashed in the end times."

"Oh no," I said, with a sigh.

"Expect signs in the sky. There will be comets, meteorites and asteroids. Earth will be rocked and will eventually tilt off its axis. Expect solar flares and geomagnetic storms. Comets will shake all things. These comets are made from rock, dust and frozen gas which orbit the Sun. As all things fall out of alignment, they will dissolve in the sun's heat, releasing dust and gases into space which will stretch for millions of miles."

"Signs in the Heavens above," I commented.

"As you have seen meteorites will crash into earth. These meteorites can be small and will plummet in large numbers, leaving fire trails in the sky behind them. Fires will start and extensive damage will be inflicted by their impact."

"I hope it doesn't get worse," I said.

"The most terrifying period will be during the sounding of the second and third trumpets," said the angel. "A mountain and a great star will fall to earth. Asteroids are objects which can range from the size of a car, to the substance of an island nation. Heed the revelation: 'Then the second angel sounded: And something like a great mountain burning with fire was thrown into the sea, and a third of the sea became blood. And a third of the living creatures in the sea died, and a third of the ships were destroyed. Then the third angel sounded: And a great star fell from Heaven, burning like a torch, and it fell on a third of the rivers and on the springs of water. The name of the star is Wormwood. A third of the waters became Wormwood and many men died from the water because it was made bitter' " (Revelation 8:8-11).

"All will see them coming," I said.

"The Lord has made all for Himself," said the angel. "Yes, even the wicked for the day of doom. When Wormwood strikes the planet, the scope of this judgment will shake earth off its axis. It will throw the seasons into chaos. Before it arrives, the Wormwood asteroid will be trackable from earth. You are correct, people will know it's coming" (Proverbs 16:4).

"The impact will be unimaginable," I said.

"Think of a strike releasing an amount of energy, similar to one hundred million tones of TNT going off at the same time. It will be worse than this. All this energy in motion will be converted into heat and debris will rise into the atmosphere. It will then fall to the ground as burning hot rocks, setting alight forests and homes. Think of a ball of light falling across the sky, with its heat scorching all before it and leaving an enormous crater.

"With Wormwood, there will be enough power to destroy whole cities and create a magnitude twelve-plus earthquake. Enough dust will be thrown high into the atmosphere to block out sunlight and stop photosynthesis. The food supply chain will be disrupted as the world's temperature falls, as little sun can get through. It will be an impact winter.

"Great cities will suffer. Those cramped into high rises and shantytowns will have nowhere to escape. Cities will collapse, bridges will fall and pipes will break releasing gas to start fires everywhere. New York City will be cut off!

"Those running from buildings and sheltering in the

streets will feel the impact of glass shattering, and structures falling in every direction. When these people don't have homes, jobs, families, or access to food and water, the rule of law breaks down. Survival mode will take over. When it's a choice between your child or another dying, looting and rage will take place. Then, another crisis will follow the immediate outrage. This shocking release of power will cause tsunamis worldwide."

"Show me," I said.

"What you see you cannot unsee," declared the angel.

I saw the earth and my eyes were drawn to the West coast of Africa. In the Atlantic Ocean, I saw the Island of La Palma. A violent earthquake struck and a four kilometre crack on the southern end of the island split the island in two. Five hundred cubic square kilometres of debris rushed towards the sea.

As it hit the sea, an enormous wall of water was created and a mega-tsunami drove this tower of water away from the island. It became as tall as the Freedom Tower in New York. As the tsunami surged in all directions it shrunk in size, but its power was unstoppable, speeding at six hundred miles per hour.

Within sixty minutes West Africa was hit by the first wave, followed by Europe a few hours later. Six hours after the quake, tens of millions in the low-lying Caribbean islands ran for their lives at the flooding from the sea. Thirty minutes later the East coast of America was smashed, with the ocean surging into the cities and towns where millions of Americans live.

As the tsunami drew close to these areas it heaped up, growing faster and bigger, as the seabed condensed its power. When it hit land it was like a river in reverse, forcing in an unstoppable tide of water for mile after mile. It devastated low-lying cities and towns. Miami, Washington, New York and Boston, amongst many others, were overwhelmed. The Katrina nightmare of 2005 was nothing compared to this.

Following the main surge of water emerged smaller follow-up tsunamis. Just when the survivors felt it was safe to emerge, as the waves of water stilled, it withdrew back to the sea. As the water surged back it picked up debris and pulverized them like a battering ram into homes and buildings. This surge of water returning to the ocean prevented the military, doctors, police and firefighters from providing help. Retaining law and order is impossible in such chaos.

Everything was engulfed in the flood of water and millions died. There were too many bodies to be identified or buried, so they rotted where they lay. With human and animal corpses decaying, a biological and humanitarian nightmare commenced. The clean water supply was destroyed leading to dysentery, cholera and many infections became rampant.

All coastal ports in the tsunami's path were crushed and supply lines into the United States were severed. Efficient just-in-time deliveries collapsed and cities ran out of food within two weeks. Those left living in these cities did not have the land or the knowledge of how to grow supplies for themselves. Coastal cities were evacuated and left in ruin. The shock to the global economy led to the greatest depression the modern world has ever known. In the aftermath, cities were replaced with tented camps in the wilderness, surrounded by barbed wire fences and armed soldiers. There was no time for trials and laws. He who shoots first has power.

"We've seen nothing like this before," I said.

"You have been born in a time of freedom, in a nation that does not know what it is to live under occupation. The blessing of God has protected Great Britain and the United States. But if you delve into history, you will identify the signs of natural disasters which shook the world. If you study you will find three significant periods of God's grace followed by judgment described in Scripture:

"The first was from Adam to Noah (Genesis 6-8).

"The second was from the time of Noah to the generation which rejected Jesus (Matthew 23:16-23).

"The last is called the Time of the Gentiles, from the time of the fall of Jerusalem, till present day (Luke 21:20-28).

"Just as Sodom and Gomorrah became a symbolic warning to every generation, in the same manner, the

Time of the Gentiles began with several warnings.

"On 24 August AD 79, an eruption from the volcano Vesuvius turned a great city into an ash heap. After the eruption, the cloud was so dense it turned day to night. What followed was a downpour of fine ash, pumice, rock and solidified lava hurtling toward people.

"A twenty mile high plus column of debris spurted out of the volcano, until part of it collapsed. Then a pyroclastic current of debris surged down the mountain towards the inhabitants below. In less than five minutes a wave of searing burning gas and ash struck Herculaneum, and its people died instantly. A pyroclastic current struck them, turning their flesh into vapour in the intense heat. With the debris from the volcano, people were turned into ash and it burnt their bones within seconds."

"God have mercy," I said.

"This pyroclastic surge slowed before Pompeii. It cooled down to such an extent that it did not vaporise people's flesh there. Yet it rushed in like a tsunami and people died instantly. Still falling upon the city was layer upon layer of thick ash and pumice. The rich and the poor, the slave and the free died together. These people were not suffocated by falling ash or burnt alive by lava; instead, they were struck down by the intense heat of pyroclastic surges. Then Pompeii was buried under a thick blanket of volcanic ash and the city was frozen in time, as an example to all who have ears to hear and eyes to see.

"In this Roman city, time stopped. Over time, the ash which concealed the bodies of the inhabitants of Pompeii hardened and encased them in a rigid outer shell, freezing their positions. As their flesh decomposed, a cavity was left inside the shell and almost two thousand years later, archaeologists pumped plaster into these shells to develop casts of those who died."

"What a terrible time to be alive," I said.

"God has given signs and warnings in your generation," said the angel. "On Sunday 18 May 1980, after 123 years of inactivity, Mount St. Helens erupted violently and it sent half a billion tons of ash and debris across three states. This was the deadliest and most costly volcanic event in American history.

"A pyroclastic current of a searing hot avalanche of ash and dust exploded down the side of the mountain. Inside the debris temperatures measured seven hundred degrees Celsius and the gas travelled at nearly one hundred and thirty kilometres per hour. It obliterated everything for over six miles in its path.

"Fifteen miles of railways were destroyed, plus forty-seven bridges, one hundred and eighty-five miles of roads and two hundred and fifty homes were lost. It was a lateral collapse; it erupted sideways instead of upwards, as the volcano turned from a solid mass into a pile of rocks thundering downwards.

"This was not the first sign for America. On 18 April 1906, the San Francisco earthquake struck the coast of Northern California, with a magnitude close to eight. The devastating fires which followed consumed eighty percent of the city of San Francisco, with three thousand deaths. Out of a population of nearly 400,000, up to 300,000 became homeless.

"The signs of the times and the beginning of the troubles are echoed in history, and have no geographic boundary. On Boxing Day 2004, nearly 250,000 people were killed in southern Asia in a devastating tsunami, which also struck as far as Africa. On 11 March 2011, Japan was also struck by a tsunami and a nuclear catastrophe was only just spared. Japan is the best-prepared country in the world for such an event and yet they were caught out, and a nuclear meltdown was narrowly avoided.

"When these terrible times come to the end time generation, people will put their faith in Antichrist to help them, but even he will fail as it gets worse. Those who place their faith in Antichrist must be judged.

"With the sounding of the fifth trumpet, Satan will be given the power to release hoards of demonic beings from the bottomless pit to torment all who are not under God's protection. Those who repent during this time and express faith in Christ will be protected from this evil attack" (Revelation 9:1-4, 11).

Chapter Twenty-Six

Armageddon

In the final surge to overwhelm Israel, I continued to see waves of planes, tanks, drones and unlimited soldiers flooding in. Their borders to the north and east were overwhelmed, and the battle of the ages was taking place. Nuclear explosions rained down upon the Middle East – but not on Israel – as God's chosen nation used everything it possessed to survive.

The Battle of Armageddon was bitter. Demonic hatred motivated the Antichrist armies, but the Jewish nation maintained a greater incentive – survival. It was a David and Goliath moment, and the former fought like an enraged lion. But the sheer number of Antichrist's forces was overwhelming.

"Do you perceive what you see?" asked the angel.

"Armageddon," I said.

"You have not lived through an end of civilisation event," said the angel. "Many in history have. Empires, unions, nations and civilisations fall and break apart. The peoples of ancient Persia, Egypt and Rome discovered what it means to observe their civilisation fall apart; it has happened many times.

"Europe was rocked by the fall of the Roman Empire. Christians of that age could not understand why Rome fell in AD 410. Everything changed when Roman authority withdrew and in provinces such as Britannia, it created a void which was never filled for centuries. In response to Rome's fall, St Augustine preached the city was not eternal, but instead believers are citizens of the true eternal Kingdom of God.

"Those who lived in the Byzantine, Ottoman or European Empires of the past understand what it means for the world they knew to suddenly end. Even in your lifetime, citizens of the Soviet Union lived in fear as their empire crumbled into poverty, lawlessness and decay."

"We have been blessed to escape such trouble," I said.

"Too many have fallen asleep without Christ in the comfort of a warm bed," said the angel. "Better to live without temporal comfort for a brief season, than to live forever without eternal life. Listen to me again! All which has a beginning has an end. The Times of the Gentiles will end when the Antichrist tries to annihilate the nation and people chosen by God.

"You have seen the Antichrist army invading Israel and the Man of Sin inside the Third Temple. He thinks he is in charge. But God has allowed this in preparation for Armageddon.

"Several times in Scripture God declares He will bring the nations to a gigantic battle to judge the wicked. This is what the Sovereign Lord God says to them: 'Why do you conspire against the Lord? He will make an utter end of it' " (Isaiah 34:1-17, Joel 3:2, Nahum 1:9, Zechariah 3:14:1-7, 12-15, Revelation 6:1-17).

"What should the nations expect?" I asked.

"In His righteousness, God will send judgment on the nations for their ill-treatment of His people Israel," said the angel. "He will also punish those who persecuted His saints. The Lord said, 'My determination is to gather the nations to My assembly of kingdoms, to pour on them My indignation, all My fierce anger. All the earth shall be devoured with the fire of My jealousy' (Zephaniah 3:8).

"Demonic beings have been fermenting hatred for Israel and will cause the nations to lose all sense, when they attack God's chosen nation. Satan will use liars to manipulate many: 'And I saw three unclean spirits like frogs coming out of the mouth of the dragon, out of the mouth of the Beast, and out of the mouth of the False Prophet.' Frogs make repetitive croaking in the darkness; it goes on ceaselessly and everyone will hear. This is John perceiving demonic propaganda" (Revelation 16:13).

"This is why believers need to reject the worldly narrative," I said.

"In modern times the Church has witnessed the restoration of the State of Israel," said the angel. "In this nation, there's been growth, development and expansion.

But God has not forgotten how the Jews were treated before and punishment must come. The Lord says, 'I will also gather all nations and bring them down to the Valley of Jehoshaphat, and I will enter into judgment with them there on account of My people, My heritage Israel, whom they have scattered among the nations; they have also divided up My land' (Joel 3:1-2).

"This time of end time judgment is designated as the Day of the Lord. The Bible says, 'For the Day of the Lord is coming, for it is at hand.' In his last push, the Antichrist army will build up its forces in the north beyond the borders of Israel and will scorch the earth, as it descends like a plague of locusts (Joel 2:1-3, 20).

"The Antichrist army will not be filled with amateurs; it will be trained and disciplined. It will possess unlimited foot soldiers and advanced military technology. Their planes will fly over the mountains of the Middle East to bomb the Jews. The Bible has predicted this: 'Over mountaintops they leap, like the noise of a flaming fire that devours the stubble' (Joel 2:5).

"The State of Israel will use everything in its power to resist the enemy, as their technology will not be jammed by the Antichrist forever. This includes the Samson Option of nuclear retaliation: 'And this shall be the plague with which the Lord will strike all the people who fought against Jerusalem: Their flesh shall dissolve while they stand on their feet, their eyes shall dissolve in their sockets and their tongues shall dissolve in their mouths' (Zechariah 14:12).

"Israel will fight with honour, but it will not be capable to restrain such overwhelming forces. After the Samson Option of nuclear retaliation is fully exhausted, this crisis will bring Israel to the only other option, seeking the Lord. It will rend its heart before the Lord and the Holy Spirit will be poured out upon them (Joel 2:12-17, 28-31).

"When all hope seems lost, salvation will come to Israel in the physical and spiritual realms. The Bible says, 'For in Mount Zion and in Jerusalem there shall be deliverance...The Lord also will roar from Zion and utter His voice from Jerusalem; the Heavens and earth will shake; but the Lord will be a shelter for His people and the strength of the children of Israel' (Joel 2:32, 3:17).

"God will stand up for His people Israel and will judge those who worship another spirit. He will distinguish between those who loved and served Him, and those who served other gods: 'Indeed, what have you to do with Me, O Tyre and Sidon, and all the coasts of Philistia? Will you retaliate against Me? But if you retaliate against Me, swiftly and speedily I will return your retaliation upon your own head' (Joel 3:4).

"The Lord will also save believers in Christ in the nations of the Middle East. The sons of Ishmael and Esau have been blessed because of the Christian witness among them, but many refuse to follow the Prince of Peace and have embraced the sword (Genesis 21:12-13, 1 John 2:22, 4:3).

"The judgment upon the followers of another 'prophet' is written, but many will repent and embrace Jesus Christ, the Son of God (Obadiah 1:18, Matthew 26:52).

"Expect armies from at least four major powers to pounce on Israel at the command of Antichrist. This will begin at the end of the first three and a half years of the Tribulation, when the Antichrist violates his treaty with Israel. Not all the nations in the Middle East will join with Antichrist. Those who made peace with Israel and walk in this peace will be saved from being drawn into this war of aggression (Daniel 11:40-45).

"This war of Antichrist against Israel will end at the climatic Battle of Armageddon: 'At the time of the end the king of the South shall attack him and the king of the North shall come against him like a whirlwind, with chariots, horsemen, and with many ships; and he shall enter the countries, overwhelm them, and pass through' (Ezekiel 27:1-29:3, 28:11-17, Daniel 11:40, Revelation 9:16-17, 16:12-16).

"This war will lead to the cost of food skyrocketing and God will respond in power with a severe earthquake, which will divide Jerusalem into three. As Jerusalem was forcibly divided by the nations, so cities of the world will be divided by earthquakes, as buildings continue to fall worldwide (Revelation 6:5-6, 16:18-19).

"Though the days will be very dark for Israel, there will

be many great successes for the Jewish nation and the Israeli Air Force will win battles: 'Like birds flying about, so will the Lord of hosts defend Jerusalem. Defending, He will also deliver it; passing over, He will preserve it' (Isaiah 31:5).

"When the enemy comes in like a flood against Israel, God Himself will strike the invading armies with confusion. He will give Israel exceptional abilities to fight back. Those who are considered weak in Israel will fight with skill (Zechariah 12:4-9).

"The Lord will not stand and observe Israel being destroyed: 'I will seek to destroy all the nations that come against Jerusalem,' and 'the Day of the Lord upon all the nations is near; as you have done to Israel, it shall be done to you; your reprisal shall return upon your own head' (Obadiah 1:15, Zechariah 12:9).

"When Israel has utilised all its weapons and is close to comprehensive defeat, the Lord will reveal to them it is He, and only He, who can deliver them: 'Yet I will have mercy on the house of Judah, will save them by the Lord their God and will not save them by bow, nor by sword or battle, by horses or horsemen' (Hosea 1:7).

"Look out for two areas of significance in this battle. Focus on Jerusalem, where Jesus will return to fight for His people. Then, keep your eyes on Megiddo, where the bulk of the Antichrist army will be destroyed."

"I've been to Megiddo; nothing is there," I said.

"They thought Megiddo was nothing but a ruin in history," said the angel, "but as you know, in 1918 the Battle of Megiddo laid the foundation for the restoration of the State of Israel. When the British General Allenby defeated the Ottoman Turk Forces at Megiddo, he fulfilled several prophecies which made it possible for the Jews to return home and establish an independent nation. Four hundred years of Islamic occupation terminated when Allenby entered Jerusalem peaceably in 1917 and the Battle of Megiddo set the scene for the end of a Muslim empire in the Middle East. What followed were European colonies and then independent states."

"What will happen to the millions of Muslims in the Middle East nations?" I asked.

"Many Arabs will be saved and redeemed by Jesus Christ, the Son of God," said the angel. "They have sought the Almighty at the wrong Door, but God will fulfil the promise He made to Abraham to send His blessing upon Ishmael. The full blessing of Ishmael has yet to be revealed upon earth. Yes, I say to you the blessing of the Prince of Peace will come upon many Muslims, especially upon those who belong to the nations who have made peace with Israel. God will recollect what they have done for good (Genesis 12:3, 17:20, John 10:7).

"To those who choose to align themselves with Antichrist and his plan to wipe Israel off the map, beware! God has said the very thing they wanted for Israel, will happen to them: 'I shall lay your cities waste and you shall be desolate. Then you shall know that I am the Lord' (Ezekiel 35:4, 10).

"It's extremely foolish to choose hatred over love and to side with Antichrist. God says, 'You have had an ancient hatred and have shed the blood of the children of Israel by the power of the sword, at the time of their calamity' (Ezekiel 35:4-5).

"Now I will share a truth which you may not understand. Not all the nations of Islam will summit, or be forced to submit to the Antichrist. I confess another truth: Not all Muslims are Muslim; for they follow not, nor seek for, the way of Islam.

"As I have foretold, there is a blessing stored up for nations who work with Israel in peace. Jordan chose peace with Israel in 1994 and there is a reward for it. Whilst Antichrist will strike many nations who will not fully submit to him, he will not prevail. The Antichrist 'shall also enter the Glorious Land and many countries shall be overthrown; but these shall escape from his hand: Edom, Moab and the prominent people of Ammon (Daniel 11:41).

"You know these lands to be Jordan and this nation will perform an important role in providing a refuge for the Jews who are fleeing Antichrist. Jesus taught the Jews will have to flee in the end times, and the Prophets Isaiah and Micah foretold they will be safe in parts of what you call Jordan. God has a plan for all nations (Isaiah 63:1-6,

Daniel 11:41, Micah 2:12, Matthew 24:16).

"There will be a time of wonder in the battle and people will question how Israel remains in the fight for so long. However, the Jews will ultimately undergo an insufferable defeat: 'When the power of the holy people has been completely shattered, all these things shall be finished' (Daniel 12:7).

"This is when Christ returns in person and every eye will behold Him. The Lord Jesus will defeat all the enemies of Israel in a supernatural display of power. The Bible says Antichrist will 'fall by a sword not of man,' and of Christ's return, 'who can endure the day of His coming? Who can stand when He appears? For He will be like a refiner's fire or a launderer's soap' (Isaiah 31:8, Malachi 3:2-3, Revelation 19:17-21).

"Make no mistake, the Antichrist is doomed. The Bible says, 'Then the Lawless One will be revealed, whom the Lord will consume with the breath of His mouth and destroy with the brightness of His coming' " (2 Thessalonians 2:8).

"Hallelujah," I exclaimed.

Chapter Twenty-Seven

Israel is Restored

"When the army of Antichrist has come close to the utter destruction of the State of Israel, God will restore the Jewish people in His nation. The veil must be taken away and they will understand Jesus Christ of Nazareth is their Messiah (Isaiah 25:6-8, 2 Corinthians 3:15, Ephesians 4:18).

"In this horrific war of attempted annihilation, Antichrist forces will massacre large numbers of the population, but God will save all who cry to Him. The work will be cut short in righteousness and a remnant will be chosen (Romans 9:27-28, 11:26-27).

"Zechariah foresaw these troubles, 'It shall come to pass in all the land,' says the Lord, 'that two thirds in it shall be cut off and die, but one third shall be left in it. I will bring the one third through the fire, and I will refine them as silver is refined and test them as gold is tested. They will call on My name and I will answer them. I will say, 'This is My people,' and each one will say, 'The Lord is my God' " (Zechariah 13:8-9).

I saw the Chief Rabbi of Israel broadcasting from a secret location to the nation. He spoke in Hebrew and I knew in my spirit it was a purer version of Hebrew than you hear in the streets of Israel. As the Chief Rabbi spoke, I heard a translation in English and I later tried to recall all the words he said. I understood the translation I heard was incapable of capturing the genuine spirit and elegance of what he said, and yet it helped me to understand what was taking place.

"These last few years have been a time of Jacob's trouble," the Chief Rabbi said. "We as a people have been demonised in the media and at the United Nations. We have been threatened and burdened beyond all other countries. Our people's suffering feels endless. The troubles of the world and Union have exasperated our enemies, leading to a battle for our very survival. In these conflicted times, our faith in money and weapons have melted away. We have found each other again, in love, mercy and peace. Our divisions have thawed, for we are all children of one God (Jeremiah 30:7).

"Amid our tragedy, the God of our fathers, the God of Abraham, Isaac and Jacob is in our hearts. Even those in Israel who have never been religious can be found praying, weeping and beseeching God for help. Something has changed in our heart since the Temple was rebuilt and defiled again. The spirit of our nation has changed and God's Spirit has returned to us. We have been humbled and broken, and we are fighting for survival once again. We have lost too many dear ones already.

"As I prayed for help, I've been meditating on the words of the Prophet Isaiah and they have revealed deep truths to me:

> 'Yet hear now, O Jacob My servant,
> And Israel whom I have chosen.
> Thus says the Lord who made you,
> And formed you from the womb,
> Who will help you:
> "Fear not, O Jacob My servant;
> And you, Jeshurun, whom I have chosen.
> For I will pour water on him who is thirsty,
> And floods on the dry ground;
> I will pour My Spirit on your descendants,
> And My blessing on your offspring;
> They will spring up among the grass
> Like willows by the watercourses.'
> One will say, 'I am the Lord's,'
> Another will call himself by the name of Jacob,
> Another will write with his hand, 'The Lord's,'
> And name himself by Israel" ' (Isaiah 44:1-5)

"This is such a time. The waters of God's Spirit are upon us. In the past we have placed many idols before our God. Idols of secular ideology, military strength, empty pursuits, to religious idols and now we must forsake them all (Zechariah 13:1-2).

"Our beloved Temple, which generations hoped and

longed for, was open for just over three and a half years! I have asked God why He allowed this and He spoke to me through the words of a Jew.

"He said to me, 'Believe Me, the hour is coming when you will neither on this mountain, nor in Jerusalem, worship the Father. You worship what you do not know; even though salvation is of the Jews. But the hour is coming, and now is, when the true worshipers will worship the Father in spirit and truth; for the Father is seeking such to worship Him. God is Spirit, and those who worship Him must worship in spirit and truth' (John 4:21-24).

"His Spirit spoke to me and told me we have put our hope in a physical Temple, but God has shown me, our bodies should be His dwelling place. I asked Him to tell me how we can be His temples and He spoke (1 Corinthians 6:19).

"He said, 'Seek the Way, the Truth and the Life,' and I said, 'Who is He Lord, that I should believe on Him?' and He replied, 'You both know Me and you know where I am from; and I have not come of Myself' (John 7:28-29, 14:6).

"There was silence as I pondered these things and I was given the courage to ask, 'What is the name of the Anointed One?'

"A Voice replied, 'He is the glory of Your people Israel' (Luke 2:32).

"But who I asked? And yet, you and I know to whom I refer! The One we dare not name and yet must. He is the most famous Jew who ever lived. He is the Suffering Servant who loves His suffering nation; the One our forefathers rejected and whose followers persecuted us in their folly of unbelief. They did not understand the Scriptures, nor did we. And yet I cried out, 'No, not Him, there must be another!' (Isaiah 53).

"Our prayers have been for our Mashiach ben David, the Messiah, the son of David. He who will gather the exiles back to Israel, restore the religious courts of justice, bring an end to wickedness and reward the righteous. When the Temple was rebuilt and sacrifices began, we looked with hope (Isaiah 2, 11, 42, 59:20,

Jeremiah 23, 30, 33, 48:47, 49:39, Ezekiel 38:16, Hosea 3:4-3:5, Micah 4, Zephaniah 3:9, Zechariah 14:9, Daniel 10:14).

"Our Anointed One must be a descendant of King David, one who loves the justice of Jewish law and he must be a great military leader. He is the one who will secure the borders of Israel, bring peace through strength and blessing will come to all the world through him. He will lead us into the world to come (2 Samuel 7:12-13; Jeremiah 23:5, 33:15, Isaiah 11:2-5).

"Then the Voice said, 'He will come to fight for Israel now if you welcome Him.'

"Who?" I asked, "as I hoped I was wrong, looking for another."

The Voice replied, "The One whom you say came for the Gentiles, but first He came for the Jews! Will you welcome Him?"

"We are desperate," I confessed. "We have no other options but to look for the promised Anointed One, whomsoever He may be."

"I knew His name, but I was afraid to speak it. His name is the name that has been on our lips, ever since the time of testing has humbled us. Our suffering has opened our eyes to see what was unbearable to see before. A broken and contrite heart has revealed His name to us (Psalm 51:17).

"His name is the name we whisper in secret and quietly we pray to Him. We have lived in fear of His name and the misuse of it; now it is our only hope. He came for the Jews first and then for the Gentiles. He is our Anointed One! His followers persecuted us and thus we rejected speaking His name because of them, but we and they were wrong (Romans 1:16).

"I was conflicted because His followers poisoned any hope in Him; they in unbelief, we in suffering. The more they hated and persecuted us, the greater our rejection became of the greatest Jew who ever lived.

"But God has spoken to me and told me that 'the gifts and the calling of God are irrevocable' and 'God has committed us all to disobedience, that He might have mercy on all' (Romans 11:29-32).

"He showed me that 'blindness in part has happened to Israel, until the fullness of the Gentiles has come in and so all Israel will be saved, as it is written: 'The Deliverer will come out of Zion, and He will turn away ungodliness from Jacob.'

"We have been under the influence of 'a spirit of stupor,' we have had 'eyes that should not see and ears that should not hear, to this very day' (Romans 11:8, 25-27).

"What has happened to Israel in this hour represents nothing less than the fulfilment of the prophecy of Zechariah: 'And I will pour on the house of David and on the inhabitants of Jerusalem the Spirit of grace and supplication; then they will look on Me whom they pierced. They will mourn for Him as one mourns for his only son, and grieve for Him as one grieves for a firstborn' (Zechariah 12:10).

"I asked the Lord, who is this One we have pierced? Is it not our nation? And the Voice said, 'No.'

"Yet I was terrified to reveal His name and now, I speak as the spiritual head of this nation, in my office as Chief Rabbi of Israel. I permit you to speak in His name, to pray in His name, and to repent in dust and ashes in His name. He is our Anointed One – His name...oh...it's too precious..."

Suddenly across Israel, I detected the sound of a Heaven-sent great awakening. The echoes of weeping, lamenting and groaning filled the streets. It was like the sound of humming and weeping together. Those who walked the dangerous streets fell slain in the road, with their bags discharging their contents. No one was still or silent. All wept bitterly, as if their only son had died a brutal death.

"His name," continued the Chief Rabbi, "is the name above all other names, the forbidden name no more! Our Jewish Messiah...our Lord God Almighty...our Deliverer...our Anointed One. He is the Son of the nation and the Son of the Most High...Oh, we repent in dust and ashes. His name is Yeshua, Mashiach ben David! Jesus, the Messiah, the son of David.

"Do not be shocked when I declare His name. He is our Anointed One. He is our Jewish Messiah. His disciples were Jewish and these Jews transformed the world. Oh, listen to the words of a Jewish fisherman who first announced the Messiah had come. These exact words transformed my heart! 'Him God has exalted to His right hand to be Prince and Saviour, to give repentance to Israel and forgiveness of sins' (Acts 5:31).

"With the restoration of Israel there will be another great worldwide blessing," said the angel, "because the Jews did not recognise their King, salvation has come to the Gentiles! But this is not the end. The promise of Scripture is the restoration of Israel will cause an incomparable blessing in revival for the Gentiles. In this end time Holy Spirit revival and great awakening, a vast harvest will be reaped. This is how Paul explains the wonder: 'I say then, have they stumbled that they should fall? Certainly not! But through their fall, to provoke them to jealousy, salvation has come to the Gentiles. Now if their fall is riches for the world and their failure riches for the Gentiles, how much more their fullness' (Romans 11:11-12).

"In the Heavenly realms, there is a gigantic battle between satanic forces of evil blinding the eyes of unbelievers and the angels of the Lord," said the angel. "When Israel is restored, an angelic breakthrough will be released into the world for a great end time harvest of souls (2 Corinthians 4:4, Ephesians 2:2).

"The Bible says, 'Then I saw another angel flying in the midst of Heaven, having the everlasting gospel to preach to those who dwell on the earth – to every nation, tribe, tongue, and people – saying with a loud voice, "Fear God and give glory to Him, for the hour of His judgment has come; and worship Him who made Heaven and earth, the sea and springs of water" ' " (Revelation 14:6-7).

Chapter Twenty-Eight

The Return of Jesus Christ

"With the restoration of Israel, the world will be ready for the return of their Messiah-King," said the angel. "When the Anointed One first came to Israel two thousand years ago, the Jewish people expected a Lion to crush Rome, but they got a Lamb. Now the Church is expecting the return of the Lamb, but they will get the Lion of the Tribe of Judah who will tread the grapes of God's wrath! Christ will return as a Conqueror and will punish all in His vineyard that resisted and rejected His will" (Revelation 5:5).

"It will be amazing," I said.

"The restoration of Israel will result in the fulfilling of a great prophecy," said the angel. "For 'none of them shall teach his neighbour and none his brother, saying, "Know the Lord," for all shall know Me, from the least of them to the greatest of them' (Hebrews 8:11).

"But before Jesus Christ can return to establish His reign in the Millennial Kingdom, as you have learnt, the Bible predicts Israel must come within a hairbreadth of a military catastrophe. The nation will experience virtually absolute occupation by Antichrist forces, until Christ returns to stop them. There are several passages in the Bible that describe these events from different viewpoints:

"Behold, the Day of the Lord is coming and your spoil will be divided in your midst. For I will gather all the nations to battle against Jerusalem...Then the Lord will go forth and fight against those nations. As He fights in the day of battle and in that day His feet will stand on the Mount of Olives. Which faces Jerusalem on the east and the Mount of Olives shall be split in two. From east to west, making a very large valley. Half of the mountain shall move toward the north and half of it toward the south. And in that day it shall be – that living waters shall flow from Jerusalem, half of them toward the eastern sea and half of them toward the western sea. In both summer and winter it shall occur. And the Lord shall be King over all the earth (Zechariah 14:1-8).

"That you may be counted worthy of the Kingdom of God... and to give you who are troubled rest with us when the Lord Jesus is revealed from Heaven with His mighty angels, in flaming fire taking vengeance on those who do not know God, and on those who do not obey the gospel of our Lord Jesus Christ (2 Thessalonians 1:5-8).

"I saw the Beast, the kings of the earth, and their armies, gathered together to make war against Him who sat on the horse and against His army. Then the Beast was captured and with him the False Prophet who worked signs in his presence, by which he deceived those who received the Mark of the Beast and those who worshipped his image. These two were cast alive into the lake of fire burning with brimstone. And the rest were killed with the sword which proceeded from the mouth of Him who sat on the horse. And all the birds were filled with their flesh (Revelation 19:19-21).

"Will you still say before Him who slays you, 'I am a god?' But you shall be a man and not a god, in the hand of Him who slays you...the Lawless One, the Lord will consume with the breath of His mouth and destroy with the brightness of His coming (Ezekiel 28:9, 2 Thessalonians 2:8).

"After these things I saw another angel coming down from Heaven, having great authority and the earth was illuminated with his glory. And he cried mightily with a loud voice, saying, 'Babylon the great is fallen, and has become a dwelling place of demons, a prison for every foul spirit and a cage for every unclean and hated bird! For all the nations have drunk of the wine of the wrath of her fornication, the kings of the earth have committed fornication with her and the merchants of the earth have become rich through the abundance of her luxury...'

"Then a mighty angel took up a stone like a great millstone and threw it into the sea, saying, 'Thus with violence the great city Babylon shall be thrown down and shall not be found anymore. The sound of harpists, musicians, flutists and trumpeters shall not be heard in you anymore. No craftsman of any craft shall be found in you anymore and the sound of a millstone shall not be heard in you anymore. The light of a lamp shall not shine in you anymore and the voice of Bridegroom and bride shall not be heard in you anymore. For your merchants were the great men of the earth, for by your sorcery all the nations were deceived. And in her was found the blood of prophets and saints, and of all who were slain on the earth' (Revelation 18:1-24).

"Daniel also foresaw the nightmare war which will be fought against Israel," said the angel. "In his revelation, he saw the Archangel Michael fulfilling a key role in the end times. He saw the defeat of an iniquitous system giving way to the Day of Judgment, the dead rising and the Millennial Reign of peace. Listen to Daniel:

"At that time Michael shall stand up, the great prince who stands watch over the sons of your people; and there shall be a time of trouble, such as never was since there was a nation, even to that time. And at that time your people shall be delivered, every one who is found written in the book. And many of those who sleep in the dust of the earth shall awake, some to everlasting life, some to shame and everlasting contempt. Those who are wise shall shine like the brightness of the firmament and those who turn many to righteousness like the stars forever and ever. But you, Daniel, shut up the words and seal the book until the time of the end; many shall run to and fro, and knowledge shall increase (Daniel 12:1-4).

"Behold, the Day of the Lord comes, cruel, with both wrath and fierce anger, to lay the land desolate and He will destroy sinners from it. For the stars of Heaven and their constellations will not give their light; the sun will be darkened in its going forth, and the moon will not cause its light to shine. Therefore I will shake the Heavens and the earth will move out of her place, in the wrath of the Lord of hosts and in the day of His fierce anger. It shall be as the hunted gazelle and as a sheep that no man takes up. Every man will turn to his people and everyone will flee to his land" (Isaiah 13:4-14).

"This sounds like Rome, the capital of the Antichrist

Empire," I observed (Revelation 17:9).

"When Zechariah saw Messiah returning to earth, the Mount of Olives split in two at His power. This will provide a path for God's chosen people in Jerusalem, who are living under Antichrist occupation to escape. In the protection of their Divine shelter, they will be safe as Christ and His armies defeat the Antichrist forces. In time, freshwater will flow through this gap purifying the Dead Sea and bringing life to wherever it flows."

"Many of the prophets saw this day coming," I said.

"John said, 'Behold, He is coming with clouds and every eye will see Him, even they who pierced Him. And all the tribes of the earth will mourn because of Him. Even so, Amen" (Revelation 1:7).

Chapter Twenty-Nine

Christ's Millennial Reign

"Every eye will see Jesus Christ when He returns with His armies to defeat Antichrist," said the angel. "When the war is over, Jesus will lay the foundation for the Millennial Reign, a thousand years of blessing (2 Thessalonians 1:7-10, Revelation 19:13-14).

"Jude said this of the Lord's coming: 'Now Enoch, the seventh from Adam, prophesied saying, "Behold, the Lord comes with ten thousands of His saints, to execute judgment on all, to convict all who are ungodly among them of all their ungodly deeds which they have committed in an ungodly way, and of all the harsh things which ungodly sinners have spoken against Him" ' (Jude 1:14-15).

"John saw these events too: 'Now I saw Heaven opened and behold, a white horse. And He who sat on him was called Faithful and True, and in righteousness He judges and makes war. His eyes were like a flame of fire and on His head were many crowns. He had a name written that no one knew except Himself. He was clothed with a robe dipped in blood and His name is called the Word of God. And the armies in Heaven, clothed in fine linen, white and clean, followed Him on white horses. Now out of His mouth goes a sharp sword, that with it He should strike the nations. And He Himself will rule them with a rod of iron. He Himself treads the winepress of the fierceness and wrath of Almighty God. And He has on His robe and on His thigh a name written: King of kings and Lord of lords' " (Revelation 19:11-16).

"We serve the King of kings!" I proclaimed.

"He is coming as the King of the Jews to fulfil the covenant God made with King David (Psalm 89:3-4).

"Under the auspices of this covenant, King Jesus has been ruling and reigning in Heaven. Upon His return to earth, He shall manifest this rule to all nations during the

Millennial Reign. God promised David this would happen: 'My covenant I will not break, nor alter the Word that has gone out of My lips. Once I have sworn by My holiness; I will not lie to David: His seed shall endure forever and his throne as the sun before Me. It shall be established forever like the moon, even like the faithful witness in the sky' " (Psalm 89:34-37).

"Please, brief me about this reign," I said.

"God is a distinguished economist," he said, "and He can fill one passage of Scripture with meaning for every age. Just think of Isaiah 65. This chapter deals with events in Isaiah's lifetime (Isaiah 65:6-12), the Church age (Isaiah 65:1) and the Millennial Reign (Isaiah 65:25). It also covers the period of the new Heavens and earth (Isaiah 65:17).

"This prophet spoke of the past, present and future all in one, just like the Book of Revelation. God resides outside of your understanding of time, and He can see the past, present and future in one glance. Therefore, one prophecy can often concern many ages or times. As Jesus said, 'Write the things which you have seen and the things which are, and the things which will take place after this' (Revelation 1:19).

"This is also the case with Jesus' parable of the talents. First, it concerns how you treat the 'least of these' on earth in your time, and second, the Sheep and the Goat Judgment of the Nations in the end times" (Matthew 25:14-30).

"It's hard to perceive the multiple meanings," I said.

"When Antichrist and His armies are defeated, Jesus will commence building a new peaceful civilisation. The Lord will begin the process with the separation of the sheep from the goats and the wheat from the chaff (Luke 3:17).

"The following people will be judged during the Sheep and the Goat Judgment of the Nations:

"One, the restored of Israel.

"Two, believers who repented during the Tribulation.

"Three, the martyred of the Tribulation.

"Four, the surviving unbelieving Gentile nations.

"As you now know, before the Tribulation begins,

Christians will be Raptured and experience the Judgment of Believers in Heaven. At the beginning of the Millennial Reign the second judgment begins, this time for the Sheep and the Goats."

"It will be astonishing to see Christ ruling," I said.

"The Sheep and Goat Judgment will take place on earth," said the angel. "To fulfil biblical prophecy, Jesus, the King of the Jews, will judge the nations at the beginning of His Reign from the throne of David in Jerusalem.

"Jesus said, 'When the Son of Man comes in His glory and all the holy angels with Him, then He will sit on the Throne of His Glory. All the nations will be gathered before Him and He will separate them one from another, as a shepherd divides his sheep from the goats. And He will set the sheep on His right hand, but the goats on the left (Matthew 25:31-34).

"The sheep will be the restored of Israel and the Gentile followers of Jesus Christ who were saved during the Tribulation period. The goats will be those who survived the Tribulation but refused to repent and rest their faith in Christ.

"But there is something deeper to perceive in the Sheep and Goat Judgment. Jesus will judge the nations. His principal focus will be on how the nations treated the Jewish people. Nations comprise of people, and the individual will have to take personal responsibility for aiding their government's persecution or support of the Jews and Israel.

"Thus, the Sheep and Goat Judgment of the nations focuses on those who lived during the Tribulation period. How they treated the Jewish people will be key. Those who forced Israel to divide their land and those who sent troops against Israel under the Antichrist system will be judged (Revelation 14:6-7, 14-16).

"But those who fed, clothed, provided hospitality and lodgings to the Jews during Antichrist's rule will be blessed. Many helped God's chosen people during the rule of Hitler; many will also help the Jews during the Antichrist period.

"There will be nations who resist the persecution of the

Jews under the Antichrist and nations who support it. The 'least of all' during the reign of the Antichrist will be the Jews. Jesus said this, 'Assuredly, I say to you, inasmuch as you did it to one of the least of these My brethren, you did it to Me' (Matthew 25:40).

"The Parable of the Dragnet also explains how the just and the unjust will all be brought before Jesus' throne 'at the end of the age.' Jesus, the Christ is coming to establish a Kingdom of peace and the lawless cannot live in this Kingdom.

"The Lord said, 'Therefore as the tares are gathered and burned in the fire, so it will be at the end of this age. The Son of Man will send out His angels and they will gather out of His Kingdom all things that offend, and those who practice lawlessness and will cast them into the furnace of fire. There will be wailing and gnashing of teeth. Then the righteous will shine forth as the sun in the Kingdom of their Father. He who has ears to hear, let him hear' (Matthew 13:40-50).

"God said He will draw people to His Kingdom: 'It shall be that I will gather all nations and tongues; and they shall come and see My glory' (Isaiah 66:18).

"It will be during this age that every knee will bow to Jesus Christ: 'Therefore, God also has highly exalted Him and given Him the name which is above every name, that at the name of Jesus every knee should bow, of those in Heaven, and of those on earth, and of those under the earth and that every tongue should confess that Jesus Christ is Lord, to the glory of God the Father' (Philippians 2:9-11).

"To prepare for God in Christ to dwell with His people on earth for a thousand years, the Lord will purge all who are not worthy to live in His Kingdom on earth (Ezekiel 20:38).

"Christ will also raise from the dead believers who were executed during the Tribulation by the Antichrist, but the rest will remain dead until the Great White Throne Judgment after the Millennial Reign.

"For the Kingdom of Peace to succeed, two things will have to happen. First, Jesus will rule with a rod of iron to end all war and Satan will be bound for a thousand years.

Isaiah prophesied: 'He will not fail nor be discouraged, till He has established justice in the earth' (Isaiah 42:4).

"This was John's revelation: 'Then I saw an angel coming down from Heaven, having the key to the bottomless pit and a great chain in his hand. He laid hold of the dragon, that serpent of old, who is the Devil and Satan, and bound him for a thousand years; and he cast him into the bottomless pit, and shut him up, and set a seal on him, so that he should deceive the nations no more till the thousand years were finished. But after these things he must be released for a little while. And I saw thrones, and they sat on them and judgment was committed to them. Then I saw the souls of those who had been beheaded for their witness to Jesus and for the Word of God, who had not worshipped the Beast or his image, and had not received his mark on their foreheads or on their hands. And they lived and reigned with Christ for a thousand years. But the rest of the dead did not live anew until the thousand years were completed. This is the first resurrection. Blessed and holy is he who has part in the first resurrection. Over such the second death has no power, but they shall be priests of God and of Christ, and shall reign with Him a thousand years' (Revelation 20:1-6).

"The Millennial Reign will prove God's original plan for a peaceful and prosperous earth could have been before. After the Sheep and Goat Judgment, only believers will remain on earth. They will live as close as possible to an Eden-like state because Satan will be locked up. People will love to go to Jerusalem, for 'a highway shall be there and a road and it shall be called the Highway of Holiness' (Isaiah 35:8).

"Those who survive the Tribulation and the Sheep and Goat Judgment will still have bodies of flesh and blood, and the carnal nature inherited from Adam. However, they will be clothed with the righteousness of Christ, and God's presence will subdue the curse on the earth and the Adamic nature (Romans 8:21).

"Children of flesh and blood will continue to be born during the thousand year reign and they will be raised in an age which loves holiness. During Jesus Christ's reign, there will ultimately be no sickness and those born with infirmities before His reign will be healed. Jesus will go on a healing tour at the beginning of His reign to help all in need. It will be reminiscent of the occasions in the Gospels when everybody who came to Christ was healed (Matthew 8:16, Mark 6:56, Luke 4:40, 9:11).

"Isaiah foresaw this time: 'Then the eyes of the blind shall be opened and the ears of the deaf shall be unstopped. Then the lame shall leap like a deer and the tongue of the dumb sing' (Isaiah 35:5-6).

"Deserts will be transformed into harvest fields, and the wilderness into rivers and pools. This will be a time of immense joy and singing. The lion and the lamb will dwell together, and a little child will be unharmed in the presence of all animals and reptiles. Thus, wild animals will no longer be 'wild' by nature. Animals will not kill each other for food, but will find all they need for nourishment from the earth (Isaiah 11:6-9, 35:1-6).

"Israel will be the head of the nations and there will be no poverty because the presence of the Lord will provide blessing on everything (Deuteronomy 28:13, Micah 4:4, Joel 2:18-27).

"The nature of the Middle East will also change when Jesus Christ comes to establish the Millennial Reign. The Kingdom of Israel will expand and the blessed of Lebanon will be welcomed (Ezekiel 47:13-48:29, Isaiah 35:8).

"The Bible also says, 'In that day there will be an altar to the Lord in the midst of the land of Egypt, and a pillar to the Lord at its border...in that day Israel will be one of three with Egypt and Assyria — a blessing in the midst of the land, whom the Lord of hosts shall bless, saying, "Blessed is Egypt My people, and Assyria the work of My hands, and Israel My inheritance" ' (Isaiah 19:19, 24).

"God's promises for this age are beautiful: 'I will return to Zion and dwell in the midst of Jerusalem. Jerusalem shall be called the City of Truth, the Mountain of the Lord of hosts, the Holy Mountain...many peoples and strong nations shall come to seek the Lord of hosts in Jerusalem and to pray before the Lord' " (Zechariah 8:3, 22).

"It sounds magnificent," I expressed with joy.

"Man has tried to establish his Millennial Reign and it has borne nothing but misery upon the world. Now with Christ's feet on earth, the spiritual veil over the nations will be removed (Isaiah 25:7).

"There will be wave after wave of miraculous cases of healing, as many permanent injuries will be restored through creative miracles. When the Lord travels through an area, His presence will conduct the creative process, and bend death and decay to His will. The lame will walk and the deaf will hear, as the deserts are reclaimed and turned into fertile fields (Isaiah 35:5-7, Ezekiel 36:27-30).

"Jerusalem will become the administrative centre for the world and only the holy will live in the city. It won't be a gigantic city, but it will be powerful. Food will be abundant and supplies will overflow of everything. All will accomplish their calling and all work will be fulfilling (Isaiah 4:2-3).

"God's will and His physical presence will accomplish all this: 'For the earth shall be full of the knowledge of the Lord, as the waters cover the sea' (Isaiah 11:9).

"Before the return of Jesus to earth, people will worship many false gods. These idol worshippers do not understand that the sin of idolatry has released sickness and suffering in the world, because Satan comes only to steal, kill and destroy. Thus, the act of idolatry releases a curse upon them and others. But in the Millennial Reign, these false gods will be abandoned and God's blessing will not be hindered, flowing into all things" (John 10:10).

"It sounds like the best time to live," I said.

"During the Millennial Reign Christ will prove humanity could have lived in peace, harmony and joy; if only all had submitted to Him beforehand," said the angel. "He shall declare peace to the nations; His dominion shall be from sea to sea (Zechariah 9:10).

"The world will finally discover what could have been, if ancient Israel had not asked for a king. When Saul became King of Israel, the Israelites aborted God's original plan for the Kingdom of Israel to be a light to the world, without copying their structures of leadership" (1 Samuel 8:5).

"Will Jerusalem be rebuilt?" I asked.

"It will have to be," replied the angel. "The Third Temple will be damaged during Armageddon and a new Temple of the Lord will be built, with the design given by God. The Temple prophesied by Ezekiel was never built because the Lord did not desire it to be established during the reign of man. God designed it for Christ during the Millennial Reign. There will never be a blood sacrifice in the Fourth Temple because the Lamb of God has made atonement.

"The sacrifice offered in the Fourth Temple of Jerusalem will be the sacrifice of praise from the nations, who will enter the Temple to worship King Jesus of Israel and the nations on earth" (Isaiah 2:3, 56:6-7, 60:13, Ezekiel 40:1-47:1, Daniel 9:24, Haggai 2:7-9, Zechariah 6:12-15, 8:20-23).

"I didn't expect a Temple to be established in the Millennial Reign," I said.

"Both Isaiah and Ezekiel foresaw this," replied the angel. "Listen to the voice of the prophet, 'Now it shall come to pass in the latter days, that the mountain of the Lord's house shall be established on the top of the mountains, and shall be exalted above the hills; and all nations shall flow to it. Many people shall come and say, 'Come and let us go up to the mountain of the Lord, to the House of the God of Jacob; He will teach us His ways and we shall walk in His paths.' For out of Zion shall go forth the law and the Word of the Lord from Jerusalem. He shall judge between the nations and rebuke many people; they shall beat their swords into ploughshares and their spears into pruning hooks; nation shall not lift up sword against nation, neither shall they learn war anymore' " (Isaiah 2:1-4).

"True peace," I said.

"Christ, who is the true 'Branch' identified by Zechariah, will establish the Fourth Temple in Jerusalem. However, don't forget people will still be born in this time, under Adam. Thus, the Fourth Temple will be a reminder to all who are born under sin, of their need to come to the One who can cleanse them (Zechariah 6:13).

"Herod's Temple was beloved of the disciples, but they did not know the Temple revealed to Ezekiel has hidden qualities, which will only be understood when it is built. It will reveal its wonder when completed (Luke 21:5).

"Thus, the nations shall come to the Mountain of the Lord in Jerusalem and all weapons will be destroyed to establish a reign of peace. As Zechariah saw: 'Many nations shall be joined to the Lord in that day and they shall become My people. And I will dwell in your midst' (Micah 4:1-8, Zechariah 2:11).

"In this time of peace, Jerusalem shall be known as the Throne of the Lord and as I have said, the City of Truth. God will draw all to Himself to submit to His golden rule, and God's presence will enable mankind to resist the evils of the flesh and live peaceably. The Jews with their Messiah will be celebrated. No longer will they be called Israelis or any other name but the Holy People (Jeremiah 3:17, Isaiah 62:12, Zechariah 8:3).

"With all wars, famines and poverty abolished, people will enjoy an abundance of surplus wealth: 'Behold, the days are coming says the Lord, when the ploughman shall overtake the reaper and the treader of grapes him who sows seed. The mountains shall drip with sweet wine and all the hills shall flow with it' (Amos 9:13).

"As the curse of strenuous toil is subdued and abundance is produced with ease, people will possess far more free time than before. They will utilise it to celebrate God's goodness, worship the Lord and go on pilgrimage to Jerusalem: 'All nations whom You have made shall come and worship before You, O Lord and shall glorify Your name' (Genesis 3:17-19, Psalm 86:9, Joel 2:24-27).

"Isaiah describes the wonder of Christ's reign: 'His name will be called Wonderful, Counsellor, Mighty God, Everlasting Father, Prince of Peace. Of the increase of His government and peace there will be no end, upon the throne of David and over His Kingdom, to order it and establish it with judgment and justice. From that time forward, even forever. The zeal of the Lord of hosts will perform this' " (Isaiah 9:6-7).

"Many generations can be born in a thousand years," I said.

"There will be two types of people living during this age:

- 176 -

"First, there will be human beings who survived the Tribulation and those born during the Millennial Reign.

"Second, there will be the servants of Christ, the immortals who are the resurrected and glorified believers. These are the ones Christ will choose to serve with Him during His reign (Mark 12:25, Matthew 19:28, 1 Corinthians 15:53-55, Revelation 20:6).

"Thus, those of the seed of Adam will continue with their fallen nature, which will be subdued by Christ's powerful presence. Simultaneously, the resurrected and glorified believers will be the seed of Christ, the second Adam. As heirs of Christ, these resurrected believers will rule and reign with Jesus, but they will not marry or reproduce because they are like the angels (Isaiah 32:1, Mark 12:24-25, 1 Corinthians 15:45).

"Christ will delegate His authority over the nations to those believers who were found trustworthy. Jesus said, 'And he who overcomes, and keeps My works until the end, to him I will give power over the nations' " (Revelation 2:26).

"I hope the disciples of Jesus will appear," I said.

"The resurrected and glorified twelve apostles will rule and reign with Christ, as will the leaders of the twelve tribes of Israel! These two groups of people are the twenty-four elders of the Book of Revelation. The apostles will first judge and then rule over the twelve tribes of Israel, and other glorified believers will rule in various roles under them" (Luke 22:30, Isaiah 1:26, Matthew 19:28, 1 Corinthians 6:2, Revelation 2:26).

"It's beyond comprehension," I said.

"The Holy Spirit revealed to Paul that glorified believers will judge angels: 'Do you not know that the saints will judge the world? And if the world will be judged by you, are you unworthy to judge the smallest matters? Do you not know that we shall judge angels?' (1 Corinthians 6:2-3).

"There will be no wars for ten centuries and geographic changes will take place in Israel. As you have been briefed, there will be living waters flowing from Jerusalem toward the Mediterranean and the Dead Sea, at the command of Jesus, the Messiah (Zechariah 14:8, Isaiah

2:4, Ezekiel 47:1-12, Micah 4:1-5).

"God the Father will empower Jesus to establish His reign: 'But to the Son He says: "Your throne, O God, is forever and ever. A sceptre of righteousness is the sceptre of Your Kingdom. You have loved righteousness and hated lawlessness. Therefore God, Your God, has anointed You with the oil of gladness more than Your companions" ' (Hebrews 1:8-9).

"Another foreshadowing explains how praise and worship will release abundance in the earth: 'Let the peoples praise You, O God; let all the peoples praise You. Oh, let the nations be glad and sing for joy! For You shall judge the people righteously and govern the nations on earth. Then the earth shall yield her increase. God, our own God, shall bless us and all the ends of the earth shall fear Him' " (Psalm 67:3-7).

"Should we expect to see Abraham, Isaac and Jacob on earth during this time?" I asked.

"Jesus said, 'Before Abraham was I am.' He also said Abraham looked for His coming. Therefore, the covering the believer receives by faith in Jesus is also applied to Abraham and the Old Testament saints" (Isaiah 26:19, Daniel 12:2, John 8:56-58).

"It's astonishing," I said.

"You expect to see the Old Testament saints in Heaven," said the angel. "Why then are you surprised to learn you will see them on earth? Listen to Job speaking about seeing the Lord Jesus on earth: 'For I know that my Redeemer lives and He shall stand at last on the earth; and after my skin is destroyed, this I know, that in my flesh I shall see God' (Job 19:25-26).

"When the Lord travels to an area of His Kingdom on earth, creation will spring before Him. Flowers of immense colours will birth in seconds before His convoy, harvests will multiply and citizens of the Kingdom will be thrilled to welcome their King."

Chapter Thirty

The Battle of Gog and Magog
Satan's Ultimate Defeat

"During the Millennial Reign, God's physical presence enables the curse on the earth and the carnal nature inside of man to be subdued for a season," said the angel. "However, Jesus Christ will not presently undo the original curse on earth which happened because of the fall of man. The full redemption of all things will take place later (2 Peter 3:12, Revelation 21:1).

"For those who survive the Tribulation and their descendants, the processes of life will go on. They will continue to experience childbirth and death because they still reside in the mortal Adamic body. However, their lives will be extended and one who dies at one hundred years old will be considered a child (Isaiah 65:20, Romans 7:24, 1 Corinthians 15:53).

"This extended lifespan will be granted so the world can be replenished after the large death toll during the Tribulation and Battle of Armageddon. Prosperity and fertility will increase, and the pain of childbirth will be significantly reduced, which will lead to rapid population growth" (Isaiah 65:20-26).

"It's strange to think of death during the Millennial Reign," I said.

"When someone dies there will be no weeping," said the angel, "because all who die in faith will be promptly transferred into Heaven with God the Father. This is the blessing of Christ's nearness."

"Heaven will still exist at this point!" I said.

"Yes," said the angel. "Jesus is on earth and God the Father is in Heaven. Remember, those who come back to life during the Millennial Reign are raised in the First Resurrection. The others, the dead of history, will not be brought back to life until the Great White Throne Judgment at the end of all things. This is what the

Scriptures say: 'But the rest of the dead did not live again until the thousand years were finished. This is the first resurrection. Blessed and holy is he who has part in the first resurrection. Over such the second death has no power, but they shall be priests of God and of Christ, and shall reign with Him a thousand years' (Revelation 20:5-6).

"As you now know, during the thousand year reign of Christ many generations of children will be born and live in peace. However, it is God's will to allow Satan to be released again and he will steer people toward sin; notably the peoples of the nations of Gog and Magog" (Isaiah 65:20, Revelation 20:7).

"Released!" I jabbered, in concern.

"The Lord will allow the devil to be set free to test the heart of the generations who have lived under Christ's rule in peace. Despite all the blessing of the Millennial Reign, the hearts of some will turn aside from the Lord and Satan will deceive them. This is what the Bible states of this time, 'Now when the thousand years have expired, Satan will be released from his prison and will go out to deceive the nations which are in the four corners of the earth, Gog and Magog, to gather them together to battle, whose number is as the sand of the sea' " (Revelation 20:7-8).

"Satan's release is still a mystery," I said.

"Jerusalem will be the praise of the whole earth during the Millennial Reign. But mankind has always had free will. They must choose to submit to Christ or rebel. Therefore, Satan will be allowed to work his evil and manipulate the sinful nature inside the people of Gog and Magog, to cause the last great rebellion against God.

"The Lord knows some will offer Jesus Christ lip service during His rule on earth, but they will refuse Him in their heart. Satan will work on this carnal nature to deceive them. When some of mankind sides with Satan once more, they will lay the foundation for the last end time battle."

"Armageddon is not the end!" I said.

"The Battle of Armageddon was waged to defeat Antichrist, his armies and to bind Satan for a thousand years, to prepare for the Millennial Reign," said the angel. "The battle of Gog and Magog will be the climactic battle on earth to finish the rebellion of the Adamic nature!"

"Who are Gog and Magog?" I inquired.

"There will be an evil alliance between the rebels of Iran, Libya, Sudan, Ethiopia, Russia and China. But remember, boundaries and maps have changed many times in history. Expect people to join this army of multitudes from unanticipated places and the peoples of the coastlands will allow the enemy to pass through their territory to Israel" (Ezekiel 38:4-6, 39:1-11).

"The last battle!" I said, in awe.

"A thousand years is a very long time for humanity," said the angel, "and many people will possess no living memory of the rule of Antichrist or the Battle of Armageddon. It will all be ancient history to those born after these events. Therefore, Satan will deceive people into imagining they can have better lives, without submitting to the leadership of Jesus Christ from Israel.

"Once again they will lust for wealth, seeking to reclaim power through possessions and fight for supremacy, rather than finding peace in the Lord. It will be an innocent holy age and the sinful nature in some will lust for the worldly catastrophic, relentless technological advancement of the previous age. Some will desire the perversions of the Babylonian system and will seek to regain the 'right' to use and exploit people."

"It's so sad," I declared.

"After the Battle of Armageddon, Jesus Christ will teach the world to resolve its disagreements without war," said the angel. "The shocking nuclear destruction and catastrophic natural disasters of that generation will lead to a change of heart. The Lord will govern the nations into a period of total disarmament. Never again will modern weapons be produced. All the money squandered on war will be employed to build prosperous nations.

"But at the end of the Millennial Reign, Satan will encourage the rebels of Gog and Magog to rearm, but they will not retain the knowledge to rebuild weapons of mass destruction. The last war on earth will be a preindustrial war of swords, bows and horses."

"Medieval in nature!" I said.

"These rebels will think they can defeat Israel and the Messianic Kingdom because it will be a nation without walls or weapons. In this last battle, they will end the era of Christ's peace on earth and their motivation is clear: 'On that day it shall come to pass that thoughts will arise in your mind and you will make an evil plan: You will say, "I will go up against a land of unwalled villages; I will go to a peaceful people, who dwell safely, all of them dwelling without walls and having neither bars nor gates to plunder them" ' (Ezekiel 38:10).

"In the Battle of Armageddon, the armies of the world came at the command of Antichrist and they entered Jerusalem by force, and Antichrist proclaimed himself god in the Third Temple. But in the Battle of Gog and Magog, the majority of this evil alliance will fall in the mountains of Israel by Divine power. However, some forces will surround Jerusalem with the saints inside. But God's fire will fall on them" (Ezekiel 39:4, Revelation 20:9).

"It's madness to unleash war after a thousand years," I said.

"The Bible predicts the Messianic Kingdom of Jesus will not need a rearmed military to defeat the enemy at the last battle. Instead, there will be Divine intervention! Expect flooding, hailstones, fire and brimstone, which will cause utter confusion and the invaders will turn on each other. Listen to Ezekiel:

"Then you will come from your place out of the far north, you and many peoples with you, all of them riding on horses, a great company and a mighty army. You will come up against My people Israel like a cloud, to cover the land...And it will come to pass at the same time, when Gog comes against the land of Israel, that My fury will show in My face...there shall be a great earthquake in the land of Israel and all men who are on the face of the earth shall shake at My presence. The mountains shall be thrown down, the steep places shall fall and every wall shall fall to the ground.

"I will call for a sword against Gog throughout all My

mountains. Every man's sword will be against his brother. And I will bring him to judgment with pestilence and bloodshed; I will rain down on him, on his troops, and on the many peoples who are with him, flooding rain, great hailstones, fire, and brimstone (Ezekiel 38:15-22).

"This Divine intervention will defeat the armies of Gog and Magog. When it is over, the people of Israel will use their enemies' weapons for firewood and will bury the dead for seven months:

"Son of man, prophesy against Gog...you shall fall upon the mountains of Israel, you and all your troops and the peoples who are with you...And I will send fire on Magog and on those who live in security in the coastlands. Then they shall know that I am the Lord. Then those who dwell in the cities of Israel will go out and set on fire and burn the weapons, both the shields and bucklers, the bows and arrows, the javelins and spears; and they will make fires with them for seven years. They will not take wood from the field nor cut down any from the forests, because they will make fires with the weapons; and they will plunder those who plundered them, and pillage those who pillaged them.

"It will come to pass in that day that I will give Gog a burial place there in Israel, the valley of those who pass by east of the sea; and it will obstruct travellers, because there they will bury Gog and all his multitude. Therefore, they will call it the Valley of Hamon Gog. For seven months the house of Israel will be burying them, in order to cleanse the land (Ezekiel 39:1-11).

"John equally saw the defeat of Gog and Magog, alongside the ultimate defeat of Satan, with his insights concerning Jerusalem, 'They went up on the breadth of the earth and surrounded the camp of the saints and the beloved city. And fire came down from God out of Heaven and devoured them. The devil, who deceived them, was cast into the lake of fire and brimstone where the Beast and the False Prophet are. And they will be tormented day and night forever and ever' " (Revelation 20:7-10).

"At last!" I said.

"The Battle of Gog and Magog will end with Satan and

his armies being thrown into Hell. The devil will suffer torment along with those formally defeated at the Battle of Armageddon – the Beast and the False Prophet. Never again will there be war. The days of mankind's rebellion against God will be finished. The Adamic nature will have been weighed in the balance and found wanting. No more will mankind choose the way of rebellion!

"Now, at this stage, there are only four things left in God's prophetic clock to complete all things!

"First, the Great White Throne Judgment.

"Second, Death and Hades will be cast into the lake of fire.

"Third, the end of the heavens and earth.

"And fourth, the creation of the new Heavens and earth, in which righteousness dwells" (Revelation 20:11-15, 21:1-25).

Chapter Thirty-One

Great White Throne Judgment

"After the final battle of Battle of Gog and Magog, Satan will be forever defeated, never to return and all his demons will be punished with him," explained the angel (James 2:19, 2 Peter 2:4, Jude 6, Revelation 9:11, 20:7-10).

"Hallelujah!" I exclaimed.

"The First Resurrection of believers' bodies will take place at the genesis of the Millennial Reign, transporting the saints back to reign with Christ. At this point, the Second Resurrection will take place."

"That will be something to observe!" I said.

"All the unbelievers from history will be raised from the dead to experience the last judgment," stated the angel. "This is termed the Great White Throne Judgment, which leads to the Resurrection to Life or Condemnation: 'Then I saw a great white throne and Him who sat on it, from whose face the earth and the Heaven fled away. And there was found no place for them. And I saw the dead, small and great, standing before God, and books were opened. And another book was opened, which is the *Book of Life*. And the dead were judged according to their works, by the things which were written in the books. The sea gave up the dead who were in it, and Death and Hades delivered up the dead who were in them. And they were judged, each one according to his works. Then Death and Hades were cast into the lake of fire. This is the second death. And anyone not found written in the *Book of Life* was cast into the lake of fire' " (Revelation 20:11-15).

"Where else in the Bible does it note these events?" I asked.

"Jesus said, 'For the Father judges no one, but has committed all judgment to the Son...most assuredly, I say to you, he who hears My word and believes in Him who sent Me has everlasting life, and shall not come into judgment, but has passed from death into life.'

"Do you see what Jesus is saying?" asked the angel.

"Christians will 'not come into judgment' to experience the Great White Throne Judgment because they have already passed from death to life. Heed the teaching of the Lord about the judgment of unbelievers in the last days: 'Jesus said, 'Most assuredly, I say to you, the hour is coming and now is, when the dead will hear the voice of the Son of God; and those who hear will live. For as the Father has life in Himself, so He has granted the Son to have life in Himself and has given Him authority to execute judgment also, because He is the Son of Man. Do not marvel at this; for the hour is coming in which all who are in the graves will hear His voice and come forth – those who have done good, to the Resurrection of Life, and those who have done evil, to the Resurrection of Condemnation' (John 5:22-29, Acts 10:42).

"In the judgment to follow God will expose that some of the heroes of history were actually the wicked. No one will get away with their hidden sin. Jesus said, 'For there is nothing covered that will not be revealed, nor hidden that will not be known. Therefore, whatever you have spoken in the dark will be heard in the light and what you have spoken in the ear in inner rooms will be proclaimed on the housetops' (Luke 12:2-3).

"The Lord tells the world beforehand what will happen so they can repent and be saved. Jesus said, 'I say to you, My friends, do not be afraid of those who kill the body and after that have no more that they can do. But I will show you whom you should fear: Fear Him who, after He has killed, has power to cast into Hell; yes, I say to you, fear Him!' " (Luke 12:4-5).

"I have often wondered what will happen to the people who lived and died before Jesus came to earth," I said.

"God will deliver perfect judgment to those who have never heard of the Lord and to those who lived before the incarnation of Jesus. There is a mystery in Scripture that few comprehend; Jesus is the Way, the Truth and the Life, He is furthermore the Alpha and Omega, the beginning and the end of all (John 10:9, 14:6, Romans

1:20-32, 9:15, 10:14, Revelation 21:6).

"This mystery was revealed to Paul: 'For as many as have sinned without the law will also perish without the law, and as many as have sinned in the law will be judged by the law, (for not the hearers of the law are just in the sight of God, but the doers of the law will be justified; for when Gentiles, who do not have the law, by nature do the things in the law, these, although not having the law, are a law to themselves, who show the work of the law written in their hearts, their conscience also bearing witness, and between themselves their thoughts accusing or else excusing them) in the day when God will judge the secrets of men by Jesus Christ, according to my gospel' " (Romans 2:12-16).

"The judgment of those who have never heard the gospel of Jesus is still a mystery!" I said.

"Before thinking of those who died without hearing of Jesus, you should first concern yourself with making sure your name is fully engraved in the *Book of Life*. To whom much is given, much will be required" (Psalm 69:28, Daniel 12:1, Philippians 4:3, Luke 12:48, Revelation 3:5).

"Absolutely," I replied.

"But you are correct," said the angel, "there is a mystery known only to God. However, the Bible provides many glimpses into how the Lord will judge people who never heard the gospel. The Bible indicates many will respond to the light they received in the Old Testament times and perhaps they saw the Door, without fully knowing who He is" (Ecclesiastes 12:14, Matthew 7:1-5, 11:20-24, 12:36–37, 20:11-16, Luke 11:31-32, 12:47-48 John 5:28-29, Romans 1:20-21, Romans 2:1-16, John 10:9, 1 Peter 4:3-6, Hebrews 11:4-40).

"It must be easier for people born in the Age of Grace," I said.

"The most important thing to retain is that God is the righteous Judge," said the angel. "It is He who knows all, understands all and judges all. The mysteries belong to Him; He doesn't share everything (Genesis 18:25, Job 38-42, Matthew 10:37, John 3:18, 1 John 5:12-13).

"John was given his vision of the Great White Throne to remind all believers of God's power and plan. He is in complete control and there is no reason to be fearful, when the King on the throne knows your name and hears your prayers."

"May I ask about the Nephilim?" I mused.

"Let me explain to you the nature of angels," he said. "Angels are ministering spirits, but they have the ability to appear like humans. When Abraham was visited by three visitors from Heaven, they were able to present themselves to him in flesh and blood bodies. They ate and drank with him, but when it was time, they returned to the Heavenlies. Many people have met angels and been helped by them, without knowing (Genesis 18:1-32, Judges 6:21, Psalm 78:25, Luke 24:4-5, Acts 12:7-10, 2 Corinthians 12:2-3, 15:39-40, Hebrews 1:4-7, 13:2).

"Angels were created by God, but a third of them rebelled in the Heavenlies. Their leader, the Archangel Lucifer, became Satan and his followers became demons. Today, they still tempt people and enter those in rebellion, influencing them from without and within. This is why Jesus Christ gave the Church power to cast out demons and free people (Ezekiel 28:12-17, Matthew 8:28-34, Mark 16:17, Luke 10:18, Revelation 12:4).

"Most of the angels who became demons continue to operate on earth or in the supernatural realm, waiting for their terrible day at the Great White Throne Judgment. God will hold them accountable for all they have done. However, a small number were locked up in ancient times because of a terrible sin!

"This crime is described in the Book of Genesis. In the time of Noah, a few angels became so shamelessly depraved, that, 'the sons of God saw that the daughters of humans were beautiful, and they married...the Nephilim were on the earth in those days – and also afterwards – when the sons of God went to the daughters of humans and had children by them. They were the heroes of old, men of renown' " (Genesis 6:2-4).

"I don't understand what this means," I confessed.

"Two groups are mentioned," explained the angel, "the daughters of humans and the sons of God! If you are unsure who the sons of God are, you can find the answer in the Book of Job. He saw the sons of God, angels, before the Lord in Heaven (Job 1:6, 2:1, 38:7).

"The Nephilim were the offspring of this hybrid human-angel relationship. The Hebrew word 'Nefilim' can be translated as 'Giants' or interpreted as 'The Fallen Ones,' from the Hebrew 'Naphal,' to fall.

"Humankind is made in God's image. Therefore, the sin of angels and humans reproducing was considered so vile to the Almighty, that these angels were apprehended and locked away from ancient times. Jude says, 'And the angels who did not keep their positions of authority but abandoned their proper dwelling – these He has kept in darkness, bound with everlasting chains for judgment on the Great Day' " (Jude 1:6).

"Did all the Nephilim die out in Noah's flood, or did their nature continue in some who survived on Noah's Ark?" I enquired.

"When the Israelites went into the Promised Land they testified, 'We saw the Nephilim there (the descendants of Anak come from the Nephilim). We seemed like grasshoppers in our own eyes and we looked the same to them' " (Numbers 13:33).

"The Nephilim's seed continues in the posterity of Anak!" I said, in awe.

"Seventeen times Anak is identified in the Bible," said the angel. "These people were tall, strong and fearsome, and what they possessed they refused to relinquish. But under God's anointing, Joshua drove them out of Israelite territory, but they survived in Gaza, Gath and Ashdod. Goliath was from Gath (Joshua 11:21-22, 1 Samuel 17:4).

"Now you can perceive why the Israelites were told many times in Scripture to keep their faith and bloodline pure. They were forbidden to marry and reproduce with the nations around them. The Bible says, 'Do not lie with the fallen warriors of old, who went down to the realm of the dead with their weapons of war' " (Ezekiel 32:27).

"I wonder if their nature continues on earth," I said. "The Nephilim legacy could help explain the discoveries of ancient distorted skulls and large skeletons."

"The Nephilim were few in number and their legacy would have been diluted by being a minority," said the angel. "However, ancient Israel was told to protect its faith and bloodline, so Jesus of Nazareth would be a pure son of Adam – as He was – to fulfil His purpose as the Second Adam" (Deuteronomy 7:3, Judges 14:3, Matthew 15:24-26, Luke 3:23-38, John 4:22, 1 Corinthians 15:45-49).

"Your own history reveals exceptionally large men have lived and some still do. Robert Pershing Wadlow, who died in the U.S. in 1940, reached 8 ft 11.1 in (2.72 m), but he was small compared to the remains of the French Giant of Castelnau, who they estimated was 11 ft 6 in (3.50 m) tall. In England, John Middleton stood before the King of England and defeated his wrestling champion. The chronicles of history declare he stood at 9 ft 3 in (2.82 m), before passing in 1623. Science also provides humanity with a verified list of over a hundred men who lived from the twentieth century, who reached from 7 to 8 ft tall. There are naturally tall people and then there's people over 8 ft whose size may contain a mystery."

"Will the Nephilim make an appearance in the end times?"

"Jesus said, 'As the days of Noah were, so also will the coming of the Son of Man be.' The descendants of the Nephilim were active and alarming in those days! Thus, in the supernatural warfare of the end, don't be surprised if something of the nature of the Nephilim is found within the Antichrist and the Second Beast!

"The Bible contains many hints about things you do not understand: 'God stands in the congregation of the mighty ones; He judges among the gods...I said, 'You are gods...but you shall die like men and fall like one of the princes' " (Psalm 82:1, 6-7).

Chapter Thirty-Two

The End of Earth

"With Satan defeated forever and all mankind awakened from the dead and judged, the greatest show on earth can begin!" said the angel. "Jesus said, 'I came to send fire on the earth and how I wish it were already kindled!' " (Luke 12:49).

"Fire!" I blurted.

"Yes fire," replied the angel. "This time it's not the fire of the Holy Spirit but the purging fire to end all things! Peter explained when this fire will come; it will follow the Great White Throne Judgment: 'But the Heavens and the earth which are now preserved by the same Word, are reserved for fire until the Day of Judgment and perdition of ungodly men' " (2 Peter 3:7).

"The world will end in fire!" I said.

"God created the world and He will end it. The Bible says, 'You, Lord, in the beginning laid the foundation of the earth and the Heavens are the work of Your hands. They will perish, but You remain; and they will all grow old like a garment. Like a cloak You will fold them up and they will be changed. But You are the same and Your years will not fail' " (Hebrews 1:10-12).

"There is much beauty on earth," I fretted.

"The planet you know is subject to a curse," said the angel. "All you think of as beautiful is only known in part. It contains within it the promise of something better. Paul said, 'For the creation was subjected to futility, not willingly, but because of Him who subjected it in hope; because the creation itself also will be delivered from the bondage' (Romans 8:20-21).

"Everything you love about earth has been restrained by the curse – therefore, an earth without a curse will be greater! There will be glorious liberty on earth during the Millennial Reign when the curse is restrained, but there is also the promise of something far more wonderful when there will be a new earth and Heavens, in which righteousness dwells" (2 Peter 3:13).

"This is a lot to take in," I acknowledged.

"It's all in the Bible," said the angel. "Listen to Isaiah: 'The earth is violently broken; the earth is split open; the earth is shaken exceedingly. The earth shall reel to and fro like a drunkard and shall totter like a hut. Its transgression shall be heavy upon it and it will fall, and not rise again' (Isaiah 24:19-20).

"Look at Peter's explanation in detail: 'But the Day of the Lord will come as a thief in the night, in which the Heavens will pass away with a great noise, and the elements will melt with fervent heat; both the earth and the works that are in it will be burned up. Therefore, since all these things will be dissolved, what manner of persons ought you to be in holy conduct and godliness, looking for and hastening the coming of the day of God, because of which the Heavens will be dissolved, being on fire, and the elements will melt with fervent heat? Nevertheless we, according to His promise, look for new Heavens and a new earth in which righteousness dwells. Therefore, beloved, looking forward to these things, be diligent to be found by Him in peace, without spot and blameless' (2 Peter 3:3-14).

"Peter urged people to embrace the end time prophecies to be motivated to seek holiness. The earth is cursed and must end. Everything which has a beginning has an end" (Ecclesiastes 3:1-8, Hebrews 6:7-8).

"The future will be great," I said.

"John saw it: 'Now I saw a new Heaven and a new earth, for the first Heaven and the first earth had passed away. Also there was no more sea. Then I, John, saw the holy city, New Jerusalem, coming down out of Heaven from God, prepared as a bride adorned for her husband. And I heard a loud voice from Heaven saying, "Behold, the tabernacle of God is with men and He will dwell with them, and they shall be His people. God Himself will be with them and be their God. And God will wipe away every tear from their eyes; there shall be no more death, nor sorrow, nor crying. There shall be no more pain, for the former things have passed away." Then He who sat on the throne said, "Behold, I make all things new." And He said to me, "Write, for these words are true and faithful" ' (Revelation 21:1-5).

"In the Millennial Reign, Christ will tabernacle with man. But in this period, the thrones of God the Father and of the Son will be on earth! It will be a new world filled with God's light in the New Jerusalem, which descends from Heaven. The Bible says, 'The city had no need of the sun or of the moon to shine in it, for the glory of God illuminated it. The Lamb is its light. And the nations of those who are saved shall walk in its light, and the kings of the earth bring their glory and honour into it. Its gates shall not be shut at all by day (there shall be no night there). And they shall bring the glory and the honour of the nations into it. But there shall by no means enter it anything that defiles, or causes an abomination or a lie, but only those who are written in the Lamb's *Book of Life*' (Revelation 21:23-27).

"It will be more beautiful than any heart can imagine: 'And he showed me a pure river of water of life, clear as crystal, proceeding from the throne of God and of the Lamb. In the middle of its street and on either side of the river, was the tree of life, which bore twelve fruits, each tree yielding its fruit every month. The leaves of the tree were for the healing of the nations. And there shall be no more curse, but the throne of God and of the Lamb shall be in it, and His servants shall serve Him. They shall see His face and His name shall be on their foreheads. There shall be no night there: They need no lamp nor light of the sun, for the Lord God gives them light. And they shall reign forever and ever' (Revelation 22:1-5).

"The new Heavens and earth will not be like the former and will never be destroyed: 'For as the new Heavens and the new earth, which I will make shall remain before Me,' says the Lord, 'so shall your descendants and your name remain' (Isaiah 66:22).

"The new Heavens and earth will be so glorious, that the old will not come to mind, nor be remembered" (Isaiah 65:17).

"What will Christians do when the new Heavens and earth are established?" I asked.

"He who was faithful with little on earth one, will be given charge of greater things on Heaven and earth two! Jesus said, 'For to everyone who has, more will be given and he will have abundance' " (Matthew 25:29).

"Faithfulness is key," I responded.

"Jesus said, 'Well done, good and faithful servant; you were faithful over a few things, I will make you ruler over many things. Enter into the joy of your Lord' " (Matthew 25:21-23).

"The Lord is watching all," I said.

"Faithfulness in the small things is what God expects," said the angel. "This life is a test to discern who is ready to be entrusted with eternal riches. If you spend your time, money and energy chasing worldly desires and wealth, you disqualify yourself from eternal treasure. But if you pay the full price in obedience, you will rule and reign under Christ in the new Heavens and earth."

"Beyond words," I commented.

"The Lord Jesus Christ said, 'To the one who is victorious and does My will to the end, I will give authority over the nations.' The promise has always been that believers will rule and reign with Christ (Romans 15:12, Revelation 1:5, 2:26, 20:6).

"As I told you before in your revelation of Heaven, there is far more to eternal life than dreaming of paradise in Heaven. There is work to be done; but with no curse on the new earth, all work will be pure joy. It's nothing to dread; it will be all pleasure. Thus, you won't be sitting on clouds, playing harps and getting bored. There is eternal life to be lived! You will finally get to do the work you were created for and love. But there are terms and conditions: 'If we endure, we will also reign with Him' (2 Timothy 2:12).

"Are you enduring as a stranger and pilgrim on earth? Do you live as a citizen of Heaven in a world which is in rebellion against God?"

"How can I be sure?" I asked.

"If you look closely, you will find two conditions mentioned by Jesus in the Book of Revelation. He said, 'To the one who is victorious and does My will to the end.' You must walk in victory over the world and do the will of

God till the end. There must be no compromise, backsliding or half-heartedness. You must be all His and live fully for Him" (Revelation 2:26).

"I fear sin will disqualify me," I confessed.

"Do not be deceived. You know the promise of endurance is tied to the overflow of the Lord's grace and love: 'and of His fullness we have all received, and grace for grace.' The grace of God, tied with your confession and repentance leads to cleansing: 'If we confess our sins, He is faithful and just to forgive us our sins and to cleanse us from all unrighteousness' " (John 1:16, 1 John 1:9).

"How long until it all comes to pass?" I inquired.

"There is inevitably a wait with the Lord," he replied, "and scoffers will be emboldened by His grace, but time will run out. Peter said, 'Knowing this first: that scoffers will come in the last days, walking according to their own lusts, and saying, "Where is the promise of His coming?" But, beloved, do not forget this one thing, that with the Lord one day is as a thousand years and a thousand years as one day. The Lord is not slack concerning His promise, as some count slackness, but is longsuffering toward us, not willing that any should perish but that all should come to repentance' " (2 Peter 3:3-9).

"The longsuffering Saviour is holding back to give people a chance to repent and be saved," I concluded.

Chapter Thirty-Three

Are You Ready?

"Are you ready for the coming of Jesus Christ?" asked the angel.

"I hope I am," I replied.

"You will need more than hope! You must be one hundred percent certain! Listen to the truth, millions of believers in Jesus are lukewarm and must repent. They need the fire of the Holy Spirit to set them alight with the burden of eternity. Jesus said, 'Enter by the narrow gate; for wide is the gate and broad is the way that leads to destruction, and there are many who go in by it. Because narrow is the gate and difficult is the way which leads to life, and there are few who find it' " (Matthew 7:13-14).

"Repentance is essential," I confessed.

"The key to eternity is repentance," said the angel. "It opens the fire doors of Heaven, it releases the Holy Spirit in power, it shakes the nations with God's joy."

"We need Heaven on earth," I acknowledged.

"Get ready now! Don't wait any longer. Put your heart right before the Lord and trim your lamp, readying for the coming of Jesus Christ, who will come unexpectedly like a thief in the night (Matthew 25:1-13, 1 Thessalonians 5:2).

"The Church can prepare for Jesus' return by fulfilling its duty in evangelism, discipleship, world mission and prayer. It must be a light in the darkness, be generous to the Lord's work and help the poor. In praying it can restrain the powers of darkness and delay the rise of the Antichrist, it should also pray for the peace of Jerusalem, blessing on Israel and for the persecuted Church (Psalm 122:6, Mark 16:15, Galatians 2:10, Hebrews 13:3).

"The Bible declares, 'To the intent that now the manifold wisdom of God might be made known by the Church to the principalities and powers in the Heavenly places...for we do not wrestle against flesh and blood, but against principalities, against powers, against the rulers of the darkness of this age, against spiritual hosts of wickedness in the Heavenly places' " (Ephesians 3:10, 6:12).

"Can we now uncover the epoch of the Lord's coming?" I asked. "I know many have tried to predict this and no one knows the day or hour, but maybe this will help with the season" (Matthew 24:36).

"You are stepping on treacherous ground," replied the angel. "God does not require you to search for the timing, but to be ready whenever He comes; this must invariably be the focus. If the prophets wish to learn wisdom listen to this – add nothing to all God has shown you. Second, do not add a time limit for a prophecy to be fulfilled, unless the Holy Spirit compels you. God will not be constrained by your timeline" (Matthew 24:45-51).

"Be wise," I said.

"Only God knows! Listen to Him: 'For I am God and there is none like Me, declaring the end from the beginning, and from ancient times things that are not yet done, saying, "My counsel shall stand" ' (Isaiah 46:9-10).

"God abides outside of the limits of human time; He sees all and knows all. Leave to God the things of God and prepare yourself when He tells you to be ready. You have been warned to set your heart aright and be holy for the return of Jesus. When He comes will the Lord find you abiding in Him, being obedient, or will He find you wasting your time and squandering your gifts? Will you misapply your life, seeking self-worth in money, possessions and status, or will you be eternally minded?" (Matthew 25:14-30).

"Oh Lord help us," I said.

"The Bible begins with the story of the first man and his bride and it ends with the second Man and His bride. In the Lord's Prayer you ask for the return of Jesus when you say, 'Thy Kingdom come, Thy will be done on earth as in Heaven.' Only with the return of Jesus can His will fully be done on earth!"

"I am excited about the return of Jesus Christ," I said, "but I must confess I fear the rise of Antichrist and the troubles ahead."

"The Bible tells you not to fear three hundred and sixty-five times in the sacred pages of Scripture. That's one for each day."

"I need to take this medicine," I said.

"You have seen Heaven and the end times, but I must return again and reveal to you the *Battlefield of the Mind*. God wants you to live in peace as you prepare for the end times, knowing He is in control of all things. The battle for peace is fought in your mind by faith."

"Another visitation!" I said.

"A revelation to help those who need encouragement," said the angel. "Now I urge you to read the Bible, God's Word and prepare. Only in Scripture can you uncover eternal truth. It is your guidebook for life and eternity. Trust nothing else but God's Holy Word."

"Amen," I said.

"Now take courage from Scripture," said the angel. "The God of peace will crush Satan under your feet shortly (Romans 16:20).

"Jesus said, 'But of that day and hour no one knows, not even the angels in Heaven, nor the Son, but only the Father. Take heed, watch and pray; for you do not know when the time is. It is like a man going to a far country, who left his house and gave authority to his servants, and to each his work, and commanded the doorkeeper to watch. Watch therefore, for you do not know when the master of the house is coming – in the evening, at midnight, at the crowing of the rooster, or in the morning – lest, coming suddenly, he find you sleeping. And what I say to you, I say to all: Watch!' " (Mark 13:32-37).

The journey continues in book 3 of the Trilogy, with the preliminary title *Battlefield of the Mind* by Paul Backholer. Also available is the prequel, book 1, *Heaven, Paradise is Real* by Paul Backholer.

Books by the Author

- Heaven: Paradise is Real (Book 1)
- The End Times: The Book of Revelation (Book 2)
- The Battlefield of the Mind (Book 3)
- The Baptism of Fire, Personal Revival and the Anointing for Supernatural Living
- Jesus Today, Daily Devotional: 100 Days with Jesus Christ
- How Christianity Made the Modern World
- Britain, A Christian Country
- Celtic Christianity and the First Christian Kings in Britain
- The Exodus Evidence In Pictures – The Bible's Exodus: 100+ colour photos
- The Ark of the Covenant – Investigating the Ten Leading Claims: 80+ colour photos
- Lost Treasures of the Bible

ByFaith Media Books

The following ByFaith Media books are available as paperbacks and eBooks, and some as hardbacks.

Biography and Autobiography
Samuel, Son and Successor of Rees Howells: Director of the Bible College of Wales – A Biography by Richard Maton.

Samuel Rees Howells, A Life of Intercession: The Legacy of Prayer and Spiritual Warfare of an Intercessor by Richard Maton.

The Holy Spirit in a Man: Spiritual Warfare, Intercession, Faith, Healings and Miracles by R. B. Watchman. One man's compelling journey of faith and intercession.

Christian Teaching and Inspirational
Jesus Today, Daily Devotional: 100 Days with Jesus Christ by Paul Backholer. *2 Minutes a Day of Inspiration.*

Holy Spirit Power: Knowing the Voice, Guidance and Person of the Holy Spirit by Paul Backholer. *Inspiration from Rees Howells, Evan Roberts, D. L. Moody, Duncan Campbell and others.*

Tares and Weeds in Your Church: Trouble and Deception in God's House by R. B. Watchman.

Historical
God Challenges the Dictators, Doom of the Nazis Predicted by Rees Howells and Mathew Backholer. Available for the first time in eighty years. Fully annotated and reformatted with enhanced photos.

Rees Howells' God Challenges the Dictators, Doom of Axis Powers Predicted by Mathew Backholer. Discover the full story of the fascinating chronicles of how Rees Howells wrote and published his only work.

Rees Howells, Vision Hymns of Spiritual Warfare and Intercessory Declarations: Songs of Victory by Mathew Backholer. Read intercessory hymns of power.

Britain, A Christian Country, A Nation Defined by Christianity and the Bible and the Social Changes that Challenge this Biblical Heritage by Paul Backholer.

How Christianity Made the Modern World by Paul Backholer. *How the Bible Inspired Freedom, Shaped Western Civilization, Revolutionized Human Rights and Transformed Democracy.*

Celtic Christianity and the First Christian Kings in Britain: From St. Patrick and St. Columba, to King Ethelbert and King Alfred by Paul Backholer. A unique and isolated expression of Christianity.

Revivals and Spiritual Awakenings
Revival Fires and Awakenings, Thirty-Six Visitations of the Holy Spirit: A Call to Holiness, Prayer and Intercession by Mathew Backholer.

Global Revival, Worldwide Outpourings, Forty-Three Visitations of the Holy Spirit: The Great Commission by Mathew Backholer.

Understanding Revival and Addressing the Issues it Provokes by Mathew Backholer. Cooperate with the Holy Spirit during times of revivals and awakenings.

Revival Fire, 150 Years of Revivals, Spiritual Awakenings and Moves of the Holy Spirit by Mathew Backholer.

Revival Answers, True and False Revivals, Genuine or Counterfeit, Do not be Deceived by Mathew Backholer.

Reformation to Revival, 500 Years of God's Glory: Sixty Revivals Awakenings and Heaven-Sent visitations of the Holy Spirit by Mathew Backholer.

Supernatural and Spiritual
Prophecy Now, Prophetic Words and Divine Revelations for You, the Church the Nations by Michael Backholer.

Heaven, Paradise is Real, Hope Beyond Death: An Angelic Pilgrimage by Paul Backholer.

The End Times. The Book of Revelation, Antichrist 666, Tribulation and the Return of Jesus by Paul Backholer.

Christian Discipleship
Extreme Faith, On Fire Christianity: Hearing from God and Moving in His Grace, Strength and Power by Mathew Backholer.

Christianity Rediscovered, in Pursuit of God and the Path to Eternal Life: What you Need to Know to Grow, Living the Christian Life, Book 1, by Mathew Backholer.

Discipleship For Everyday Living, Christian Growth: Following Jesus Christ and Making Disciples by Mathew Backholer.

Christian Missions
Short-Term Missions, A Christian Guide to STMs: For Leaders, Pastors, Churches, Students, STM Teams and Mission Organizations by Mathew Backholer.

How to Plan, Prepare and Successfully Complete Your Short-Term Mission For Churches, Independent STM Teams and Mission Organizations by Mathew Backholer.

Biblical Adventure and Archaeology
The Exodus Evidence In Pictures – The Bible's Exodus: The Hunt for Ancient Israel in Egypt, the Red Sea, the Exodus Route and Mount Sinai by Paul Backholer. 100+ colour photos.

The Ark of the Covenant – Investigating the Ten Leading Claims by Paul Backholer. Egypt, Ethiopia and Israel, 80+ colour photos.

Lost Treasures of the Bible: Exploration and Pictorial Travel Adventure of Biblical Archaeology by Paul Backholer. Discover the Exodus Evidence and quest for the Lost Ark of the Covenant.

Budget Travel – Vacation
Budget Travel, a Guide to Travelling on a Shoestring, Explore the World, a Discount Overseas Adventure Trip: Gap Year, Backpacking and Volunteer-Vacation by Mathew Backholer.

Travel the World and Explore for Less than $50 a Day, the Essential Guide: Your Budget Backpack Global Adventure, from Two Weeks to a Gap Year by Mathew Backholer.

ByFaith Media DVDs

Great Christian Revivals. This is an uplifting account of some of the greatest revivals in Church history. Filmed on location across Britain, the stories of the Welsh Revival (1904-1905), the Hebridean Revival (1949-1952) and the Evangelical Revival (1739-1791), are told in this 72 minute documentary.

ByFaith – Quest for the Ark of the Covenant. Experience an adventure and investigate the mystery of the lost Ark of the Covenant! Explore Ethiopia's rock churches; find the Egyptian Pharaoh who entered Solomon's Temple and search for the Queen of Sheba's Palace. Four episodes. 100+ minutes.

ByFaith – World Mission. Pack your backpack and join two adventurers as they travel through 14 nations on their global short-term mission (STM). Get inspired for your STM, as you watch this 85 minute adventure; filmed over three years.

Israel in Egypt – The Exodus Mystery. A four year quest searching for the evidence for Joseph, Moses and the Hebrew Slaves in Egypt. Explore the Exodus route, hunt for the Red Sea and climb Mount Sinai. This is the best of the eight episode TV series *ByFaith – In Search of the Exodus.* 110+ minutes.

ByFaith – In Search of the Exodus. The quest to find the evidence for ancient Israel in Egypt, the Red Sea and Mount Sinai, in eight TV episodes. 200+ minutes.

www.ByFaithDVDs.org

ByFaith Media Downloads & Streaming

The following ByFaith Media productions are available to download to buy, rent or to stream via Amazon Prime.

Revivals and Spiritual Awakenings
Glorious Christian Revival and Holy Spirit Awakenings: The Welsh, Hebridean and Evangelical Revivals, Evan Roberts, Duncan Campbell and John Wesley. 1 hour 12 minutes. Discover the Welsh Revival (1904-1905), the Hebridean Revival (1949-1952) and the Evangelical Revival (1739-1791), with Evan Roberts, Duncan Campbell, John and Charles Wesley, George Whitefield and others. Filmed on location across the UK.

Christian Revival and Holy Spirit Awakenings. Join revival historian and prolific author Mathew Backholer, and Revelation TV CEO Gordon Pettie, as they examine many of the powerful revivals which shook the world in seven episodes. Including the Layman's Prayer Revival of 1857, Ulster Revival of 1859-60, Welsh Revival of 1904-05, Azusa Street Revival of 1906-09, Korean Revival of 1907-10, the Hebridean Revival of 1949-52 and more! Now on YouTube.

Christian Travel (Backpacking Short-Term Missions)
Short-Term Mission Adventures, A Global Christian Missionary STM Expedition with brothers Mathew and Paul Backholer. 1 hour 15 minutes. The mission begins when two adventurers land in Asia, a continent of maximum extremes. After overcoming culture shock and difficult travel, the adventurous missionaries preach in the slums. From India they strike out into Nepal, Bangladesh, Thailand, Myanmar, Cambodia and Vietnam. The mission also touches down in the great cities of Europe: London, Paris, Rome, Dublin, Frankfurt and Amsterdam.

Historical and Adventure

The Bible's Lost Ark of the Covenant: Where Is It? Egypt, Ethiopia or Israel? With brothers Mathew and Paul Backholer. 1 hour 10 minutes. The Ark of the Covenant was the greatest treasure in Solomon's Temple, but when Jerusalem fell the Ark vanished from history. Now join two adventurers on their quest for the Ark of the Covenant, beginning at Mount Sinai where it was made, to Pharaoh Tutankhamun's tomb, crossing the Sahara Desert into the underground rock churches of Ethiopia and beyond in an epic adventure.

The Exodus Evidence: Quest for Ancient Israel in Egypt, The Red Sea, The Exodus Route and Mount Sinai. Join two adventurers, brothers Mathew and Paul Backholer, as they investigate a three-thousand year old mystery, entering the tombs of ancient Egypt seeking the exodus evidence. Discover the first reference to Israel outside of the Bible in hieroglyphics, uncover ancient depictions of people with multi-coloured coats, encounter the Egyptian records of slaves making bricks and find lost cities mentioned in the Bible.

Notes

Notes

Notes

CPSIA information can be obtained
at www.ICGtesting.com
Printed in the USA
BVHW091351221221
624599BV00014B/1229